David Cohen

HOME ALONE

HOME ALONE

Missing:
one mum,
one dad,
my sanity
... but not a sense
of humour

David Cohen

BOOKS

First published in Great Britain in 2010 by
JR Books, 10 Greenland Street, London NW1 0ND
www.jrbooks.com

A catalogue record for this book is available from the British
Library.

ISBN 978-1-907532-05-4

1 3 5 7 9 10 8 6 4 2

Printed by Clays Ltd, St Ives plc

To Aileen who bore the brunt

Memories That Don't Go Away

'Don't tell your father I'm doing this, or you know he'll go mad.'

...

'Your mother made me promise I wouldn't tell you about this.'

...

'If I find out you've been lying, God help you!'

...

'Why don't you ask your father how long she's been his mistress?'

...

'Please go to sleep, Mama.'

...

'And ask him just how many mistresses he's had.'

...

'Why don't you ask your mother how much money her father and brothers have stolen from me?'

...

'Please go to sleep, both of you.'

...

'Women have secrets, popski, and even though I would be legally and ethically entitled to tell you her secrets, if I did so, I wouldn't be a gentleman.'

...

'Please write to me. I am your only son.'

...

'Of course I will. I love you so much.'

...

'I love you too, *Maman*.'

...

'Don't keep asking when I'm coming back, David. I'm only away because your father said he'd kill me if I didn't do this.'

I don't have to summon the voices and the mixed messages from some deep, dark cranny of my mind. They're fixed into my brain, simmering away, in my cortex, in my neural networks, memories of not milk and not honey. But memories that made me.

Introduction: London 1958

'Your mother's morally incapable of being a good wife,' my father said. 'I need your help, popski. If she doesn't go to Israel, I'll be in Carey Street. Do you know what Carey Street is?'

'No,' I said.

'The street where they have the court that makes you bankrupt,' he said. 'Your mother doesn't mind me going bankrupt, but she does mind selling the bloody flat.'

'No, no, Papa.'

We were walking down the Edgware Road in central London in order to save two bus fares, as it was 'imperative' that I understood how dire the financial situation was. I was eleven years old. 'Imperative' was a word my father loved.

'I don't really blame your mother, I blame her family. They're degenerates,' my father added. My mother was a victim of the Electra complex, he added. She idolised her father. Her loyalties had always been divided between husband and family. I have a picture of her leaning her head on her father's shoulder. His wife, her mother, stares frostily out at the lens. Her family usually won, according to my father. So she couldn't bear to do the essential to help her husband avoid Carey Street: sell the one property they still owned, a flat on Mount Carmel in Israel.

'Your mother doesn't want to sell it because her father had a Turkish coffee there once,' my father sighed.

My father talked me round over the next few months, and so I helped him persuade my mother to go to Israel to sell the flat. I was a child so I didn't ask why they couldn't just put it in the hands of a local estate agent.

My mother left for Israel in August 1959. I thought she'd be gone for just a month. People always wanted to buy flats on Mount Carmel, my father assured me. She would be back soon.

I missed my mother terribly. The day after she left, my father saw how upset I was and let me take the exotic step of placing a phone call to Israel, 'as long as you talk no more than three minutes, popski. You pay for a minimum of three minutes on overseas calls.'

When the operator put me through, my mother sounded cheery. It was sunny in Haifa. I'd have enjoyed going to the beach with her. She'd be back soon. '*Je te promets*,' she said – I promise. She always spoke French to me.

I believed her completely. She had promised to be back soon. I could cope, knowing that. Soon meant a month at most, as my father had said.

In fact, she was gone for over three years.

For about three weeks, my father and I lived together in the West End, in our flat in Seymour Place. He was behaving oddly though. He would often get home very late. One night, he took me to dinner at Harry Gold's kosher restaurant and explained that commerce was hard. If he had to be home every night, he was missing out on economic opportunities. Manchester, Brighton and Scotland all offered the chance of deals. He was especially optimistic about Scotland because bank managers there had an inferiority complex towards people from London. It was 'regrettable' – another word my father loved – that Scotland was too far away for him to get back at night.

Over the next month, my father was away often. He'd ring to say goodnight from Liverpool or Brighton or Kirkcaldy in Scotland. In Kirkcaldy the bank manager had a particularly useful inferiority complex. My father laughed, 'Even if I produce music' – this was my father's way of saying he had farted – 'he gives me overdrafts because the music comes from London.'

The Scottish connection would make it possible to pay my school fees, my father pointed out. I had just got a scholarship at one of London's great schools, St Paul's, but that only meant the school reduced the fees by one-third. The bill for each term was still steep. How could he meet it if he didn't capitalise on every economic opportunity?

He had to save the family finances, something my mother was failing to do – the flat had not yet been sold. He told me that I was too old to act the baby. The heroic feat of saving us from ruin could be achieved only if he went to Scotland.

After he had left, I saw the door of the wardrobe was open. All that remained on the hangers were four shirts and one suit.

So, without ever saying it clearly, my father had moved out. And I was home alone.

In my head I could often hear myself pleading.

'Please tell me when you're coming back.'

Sometimes I even had the courage to ask that aloud.

*

Seymour Place, where I lived from the age of nine, is a very elegant street now. It runs from just behind Marble Arch, past the West London Synagogue, past the Christian Scientist Church, past the municipal swimming pool, past the magistrates court and down to the Marylebone Road. It's an interesting street with rather good shops on three blocks.

But I avoid walking down it. It brings back too many bad memories.

I was a victim of emotional abuse but I mustn't exaggerate. I wasn't left destitute on the streets of London. I had money for clothes, money for food and a roof over my head and a school to go to. My sometimes violent father didn't disappear entirely. He had an office at 57 Jermyn Street and a series of secretaries. We spoke often on the phone. If I broke my leg or needed his help in an emergency, I assumed he would be there. In fact, that turned out to be less true than I had imagined. But for the next three years, I usually saw him only once a week, on Friday evening. I also saw my mother a few times but I was essentially on my own.

That was a huge change in my life because till then I had had a normal-ish family life. My mother and father might have been unhappy but they saw themselves as a married couple. And they honoured the Jewish ritual of the Sabbath meal on Friday evenings.

The ritual was sweet.

I would get home from school. My mother was always back from wherever she had been – you didn't ask – by 5.15. She would set the table, placing two candles at the centre. She would make sure that I was properly dressed, that my trousers were clean and my tie was straight.

Then I would stand at the table while my mother lit the candles. She would kiss me on both cheeks and wish me Shabbat Shalom.

Then we would walk down Seymour Place to the synagogue. The service lasted forty to forty-five minutes. After shaking hands with the rabbi, we would go home and wait for my father.

Sometimes, but not often, my father was late. For him, too, the ritual was important. He would say the blessings on the bread and the wine, the fruits of the earth. Peace, love and harmony are supposed to reign in the family on the Sabbath even if you spent all the other six days of the week squabbling, bickering and suing each other.

And the food was good because my mother was a good cook. She made little cheese pastries called 'bureks', aubergine salad, delicious stuffed vine leaves and Wiener schnitzels.

Once my mother was in Israel, Friday evenings changed. I'd meet my father at his office in Jermyn Street at about 7.30. We'd walk across Piccadilly over to the Trocadero or round the corner to the even grander Ecu de France, where De Gaulle used to eat during the war.

If we were going to the Ecu, I assumed it had been a good week, money made and profits pocketed, or pending. My father, however, often spent the money he expected to make before he got it.

I loved the Ecu de France. Polished waiters stood with polished spoons, ready to heap onto your plate as much as you wanted from the enormous hors d'oeuvres trolley and the just as laden dessert trolley. There was no hope of keeping kosher, as they had at least twelve different kinds of mouth-watering charcuterie.

'Don't tell your mother we came here, I beg you, popski, or she'll think I'm a millionaire,' my father said. 'She lives in cloud cuckoo land – like all Romanians.'

Whatever the restaurant, Benjamin Cohen OBE would

finish the meal with a cognac. He had got his OBE for services to the Ministry of War Transport. He always tipped generously. Then he'd walk me to the bus stop at the bottom of Regent Street, give me two £5 notes and embrace me. We'd wait in awkward silence, one of the few times either of my parents was silent. When a number 15 bus turned round the corner of Piccadilly Circus, he'd relax into a smile.

'Your bus, popski,' he'd say.

I would get on and wave to him from the top of the bus and watch as he disappeared into the crowd – a small man who usually wore a double-breasted pin-striped suit and a bowler hat. I didn't know where he was going. Benjamin Cohen OBE was always vague about his movements. I knew I wouldn't see him till next week.

I got off the bus at the second stop in the Edgware Road and walked 200 yards back 'home' to Seymour Place and Vincent Court, an ugly red-brick block that had been built in 1954. There were thirty-two flats and we lived on the ground floor in No. 28.

I let myself in. The door slammed behind me. The flat had a big living and dining room with large windows, a decent-sized double bedroom and a child's bedroom. I hated the silence there when I was alone. I turned on the radio or the TV. But the noise didn't console me. I knew I probably wouldn't see any one else till Monday morning. Other than the porter.

I hated thinking about the situation I found myself in. Keeping busy was the answer. I tried to concentrate on homework, to be swotted and trotted out – Tudors and Stuarts, Livy and Tacitus. Just what did Luther think about the wine being turned into blood? If you're miserable, swot. Boys don't cry, I told myself if I started crying.

I often stared out of the window or went for walks. I would wander round Bryanston Square, Montagu Square, Portman Square, up to Hyde Park, back again. If I tired myself out, I might actually get to sleep. I'd hold intense conversations with God. Jewish boys could demand answers from Jehovah. The difference between Judaism and other religions, my father often preached, is that Jews have the habit of cross-examining God. I put God in the dock. Why had he dumped a nice intelligent twelve-year-old who was a good opening batsman and promising left-arm spin bowler? What had I done to deserve this fate?

God didn't pay much attention and He certainly didn't answer. Jehovah gave me the divine cold shoulder.

I wrote desperate letters to my mother, begging her to come back. I was amazed she didn't fly back at once. She had cooed, for years, I was 'her *cheri*', 'her *garcon adorable*', 'her *petit prince*'. She was so proud of me. *Petit prince* kept on telling her he was crying himself to sleep he was so miserable.

After my mother died, I found some of the letters I wrote to her. Their frank misery amazes me, scribbled screams from the heart. Please, please come back, they would all end. I love you. I miss you. Please write. Please answer my letters.

My mother, Dolly, often didn't reply to my letters for a week and, even then, her replies were short and matter of fact. Selling the flat was more difficult than she had imagined. After Suez in 1956, everyone in Israel was broke. One man wanted to buy but wouldn't pay the right price. Lawyers were slow. I pleaded passionately because I wanted her to come home so badly. In return, she was practical: of course she missed me, but I had to be a good boy and concentrate on my studies.

After my father left, I wrote to my mother, explaining that he had gone and I was living alone. I sent the letter express. I pictured the scene. My mother would open the letter. She'd be shocked. She'd have to read the letter again to confirm the dreadful truth. She'd take a taxi to the airport and leap on to the next plane to London. The post office clerk said my express letter would take three days to get to Israel.

On the third day, I waited for her phone call. She'd want me to know which flight she was coming back on. I'd be there at Heathrow to meet her.

The phone didn't ring; the telegram didn't come. The next day, the same silence.

Two days after that, the porter handed me an express letter that had arrived that morning. My mother was matter of fact again. She wasn't surprised that Benjamin wasn't living at home. She'd try to come back as soon as she could. Meanwhile, I was to be brave, keep the flat tidy and go to school.

I stared at the letter. Its cool tone amazed me. But the phrases were all hers. I had often heard her call my father the 'old Casanova' and complain that he was so careless that he allowed himself to be caught 'in flagrante'. She suspected he hadn't gone to Scotland but to bed with some women. He was really too old to play the Don Juan of Jermyn Street, she sniped. He was fifty-eight when she wrote this.

I saw my mother a few times during the years she was away. She came back very briefly for my bar mitzvah, the ceremony that takes place when Jewish boys are thirteen and declares you to be an adult. She was in London for no more than three days.

If you want to put it in the jargon, I suffered from maternal deprivation, paternal deprivation, internal deprivation, external deprivation and enough anxiety to keep a small team of therapists busy. I still live with some odd effects of that.

I was not just a victim because they left me. We were immigrants and, in the 1950s, foreigners were suspect.

When my parents both moved out, we'd been living in England for only four years. But I knew it was illegal for a child under sixteen to live on his own. I could tell no one what had happened. If they found out, the police and the welfare would haul me to the orphanage where they didn't have succulent trolleys of hors d'oeuvres or wonderful desserts. Four years at my prep school had convinced me that orphans would be beaten and thrashed at every possible moment. Caning seemed to be the British hobby. I wasn't going to let any one find out the truth and put me in an institution where you'd be thwacked for breakfast and thumped for dinner.

What we can't say is often powerful, and sometimes more powerful than what we can say. Sigmund Freud, the founder of psychoanalysis, argued that his 'talking cure' worked because people finally said what they had been unable to say for years. I don't think Freud is always or even often right, but that may be because, for years, I denied that being left had had any impact on me.

Moi? Far too cool, clever and collected to let a trifle like that get to me.

Trauma might bugger up those who weren't scholarship boys at a great public school, but I was above all that. Of course, I cried a bit at first, but that was before I got the hang of solitude. It had toughened me up, made a man of me. And when I started to take an interest in girls, the advantages were amazing. I never had to ask my parents if I could stay out all night. If I wanted to have girls round, I didn't have to squirrel them away in my bedroom or get

Mum and Dad out of the way. I bought a blue smoking jacket and started to smoke cheroots. Every teenager should be abandoned by his mum and dad. I could have embroidered Larkin's most famous line – 'They fuck you up, your mum and dad'. That was inevitable if they lived on the premises. Much better to have them move out. Then there is no one to cramp your style.

It took me years to see the obvious – and to admit it to myself. If you are left as a child it hurts and it damages you. The sheer ingratitude of my parents got to me. I'd done everything a child should do to be loved. I had behaved well, got good school reports, washed my hands after going to the toilet, been a decent goalkeeper, said my prayers, brushed my teeth, smiled at my aunts and uncles.

What was my reward?

To be left alone in 28 Vincent Court, Seymour Place.

Sometimes we speak now of a lost sense of community. If there was a community in the late 1950s in Seymour Place, it did not see, it was blind as a bat – or it did not want to see what had happened to me.

Many people should have sensed something was wrong – other members of my family, my school, the doctor, the neighbours, the nurses at St George's hospital where I went at one critical point, the rabbis at the synagogue that I attended most Friday evenings before going to meet my father. They included a famous rabbi, Hugo Gryn. No one noticed or bothered. The shining exception was the dry-cleaner in Seymour Place, Jeff Bell.

Jeff Bell realised that it was unusual for a boy to be bringing in his dry-cleaning. He asked after my mother, and then, after a while, he stopped asking. He was always diffident about asking me to pay. 'If you can't pay, David, don't worry,' he'd smile. But, however much he suspected, he didn't alert anyone.

I was a middle-class Jewish boy, and middle-class Jewish parents didn't abandon their children in central London.

A few things contributed to my grand – and perhaps deluded – sense of maturity, things I will explain in the course of this story. I didn't pretend to be superhuman. And being left when I was twelve did make me strange in one way. I began to panic that I was going bald. My mother had washed my hair till she left and I'd never noticed that, when you shampoo, a lot of hair falls out. I was horrified now. Every time I washed my hair, the bathtub would be full of it. How many hairs could there be on my head? Fewer and fewer. Soon my scalp would be moon bare. I'd have absolutely no hope with girls then.

I went to my mother's GP, but he told me I was being silly. Then, I saw an ad in the *Evening Standard* for a trichologist – a hair doctor.

I saved enough out of the 'housekeeping' money that my father gave me to pay for a consultation. The trichologist's offices were just off Baker Street. I had a perfectly normal head of hair but that did not bother the trichologist one bit. He wore a white coat and made me sit down in a dentist's chair. He put on rubber gloves and examined my hair strand by strand

'Oh dear,' he muttered.

I had ghastly visions of soon being the only bald twelve-year-old in the world.

Finally the trichologist sat down opposite me. He was grim-faced. He could not lie. He had rarely seen such a worrying case. He hoped I'd come in time. For £100 – at a time when you could buy a small house for £2000 – I could have the most powerful treatment hair science had yet devised. I needed the follicle cutting edge.

'Will it stop me going bald?'

'Guaranteed.'

So I gave him £20, which he graciously accepted on account.

Twice a week, he'd run an electrical device over my scalp, which tingled painfully. Then, he would shampoo me with a red goo which contained, he assured me, 'the finest amino acid-stimulating proteins'. The shampoo cost more than champagne.

Over the next ten weeks, I saved £5 out of the money my father gave me for food. And after ten weeks, the hair doctor (who had now had £70 out of me) declared he had saved my hairline. I can't contradict him. I still have a lion's mane of hair. If only therapy worked as well as hair doctoring.

If you browse in bookshops today you will find a new genre alongside the chick-lit, the dick-lit (crime fiction and/or erotica) and the lick-lit (cooking). It is called Painful Lives or Real Lives. The book trade calls it the misery memoir, that genre where victims explain how their father, mother, priest, rabbi, uncle and, very occasionally, their aunt abused them physically, emotionally, sexually and spiritually. Abuse by aunts is not a genre which has been sufficiently developed yet. And if I poke some fun at the genre, it does not mean a lack of sympathy for any victim of abuse.

It's perhaps worth asking why the misery memoir has become so successful. There are two views. The first is that we know we're lucky and we read about suffering partly to remind us of that. The second, more cynical view is that many of those who read these books are fascinated by how young boys and girls are abused. The reader must understand every last appalling instance of the abuse, so every detail must be described in ... the greatest detail. The very reputable publisher of one memoir I ghosted asked me to get the 'victim' to remember rather more of what 'Uncle

Fred' did to her. I refused and was replaced.

Memory is fallible, of course, which is why I am very grateful to Evi, my father's second wife, for lettimg me have some of his papers from which I have often quoted. I also have my own letters from the time and some other documents. I reproduce, as memoirs often do, conversations. Here, obviously, I can't be a totally objective historian so I don't claim every word I record was said at the time. But these conversations are substantially accurate.

A good misery memoir, however, should also be inspirational. Despite being unloved, hit, abused and obliged to perform unspeakable acts, the hero or heroine manages to triumph. In the very best tales, he or she becomes a therapist.

'I know how you feel,' the victim-turned-therapist purrs, 'because I was there myself.'

Well, I *was* there myself. I have wanted to write this story since the 1970s when I was in my twenties. At first I was told it was a bit too raw – there was no such genre as the misery memoir back then. Later on, the mood had changed. Now I was told my experiences were too tame. No rabbi had suggested a bit of the other while reading Genesis. I did not score high enough on the This is How Atrociously They Treated Me scale. If the story I am about to tell you is not painful enough, I'm sorry. It was very painful for me at the time – and it has affected me all my life. But I know I'm not alone these days.

It's no accident that I became a psychologist – though never a therapist. Psychologists have tended to assume that if children are neglected when they are young, they will never make up the lost ground. This pessimism seems less certain now. As with many specific questions in psychology, it's very hard to explain why some children bounce back from trauma and deprivation while others succumb and suffer for the rest of their lives. I have interviewed many of the world's great psychologists over the last thirty years. Many of them feel nagged by a dissatisfaction. Never mind the grand theories of mind and brain, or whether Freud was right, or whether we are really computers. After 125 years of scientific psychology, we still can't explain why a particular human being becomes the person he or she is, the weave and web of what it is that makes me me and you you. Why do you love caviar, playing squash and hate Dickens while your sister can't stop smoking, has one messy relationship after another, always buys her clothes at John Lewis and believes in God?

The person who will be able to answer that – and it won't be me – will deserve a Nobel Prize. (Freud was bitterly disappointed not to get it in 1928.)

I was quite old when I was left so, in terms of psychological deprivation, I was not an extreme case. I had had an eccentric but not unloving childhood. Though my father could be violent, I was often petted and praised. When I brought school reports home there were two possible responses: a slap round the ear or a slap-up meal. When I came third in class once, my father lost control. He yelled that I had come third because I was so lazy, and he hit me. My mother, on the other hand, was consistent. I did not doubt that she loved me – until she left so suddenly.

But my childhood was not odd just because my parents left me. I grew up in the midst of unhappiness. In the 1950s, adults did not speak of sex or relationships and certainly not in front of the children. If you were unhappy, you put up with it in sickness and in health, for richer, for poorer, and you certainly didn't whinge. My parents did not understand these rules and talked all the time. So I knew they were unhappy from the time I was five or six years old.

'You've ruined my life,' my father used to tell my mother.

'And you've ruined mine,' she'd reply.

Over the years, as I say, I've often thought of writing this book. I have skirted round the story and the issues it raises. I completed a doctorate on what it is that makes children laugh. I wrote a book on being a man and also one on fatherhood. I made films about child abuse and about the mental-health problems of children. But I have always avoided describing in detail what happened to me and trying to see how it marked me. I'm enough of a hack to know that that is a dangerous reason for writing a book.

But the time has come. Both my parents are dead.

This is not a book with a happy ending. I never finally resolved my relationship with either of my parents. Though much of this book is critical of them, I also wanted to write about them because they were strange and complex failures – a man and a woman who both had enormous intelligence and charm. My mother died depressed, my father died bitter. Both died strangers in a strange land – and it wasn't because of the Nazis. They chose to live in London and to stay here. Both felt they hadn't done what they might have done and hadn't been what they might have been.

I don't want to lie on my deathbed and think: Piss, I've really ended up in the same kind of jam. This book is part of my attempt to un-jam myself – and do some psychology as well. Not every child who is abused becomes an abuser; not every child who has a traumatic childhood goes under. I hope to get some clues as to why, in the face of adversity, some children thrive while others are damaged for life.

Chapter 1

Smuggling Runs in the Family

Benjamin, my father, was born in Haifa in Israel in 1908. His father was a travelling pepper merchant and amateur astronomer. For years, I was told Pepperman had been born in Manchester, which was why we had British passports. One day, as I rummaged in boxes of papers (which I often did when I lived alone), I found his passport. It said that his birthplace was Calcutta. I still don't know whether this is true.

I never found out how he had married my grandmother Safta. However he managed the marriage, Pepperman, according to my mother, led his wife a merry dance.

'*Tel père, tel fils*,' she said to me.

Infidelity – key to the Cohen genes.

After decades of Casanova-ing in the Middle East, with the occasional pause to point his telescope at the stars, Pepperman returned to his wife. He had come home to die of lung cancer.

'He died in my arms,' Benjamin said. These were the only times I ever saw him cry. 'As soon as my father died, I gave up smoking. I knew it had caused the cancer long before the doctors proved it.'

My father was an exceptionally bright child. There was a school on Mount Carmel that was run by monks and they educated him. He learned to speak perfect French and he passed a string of exams so well that the monks arranged for him to go to Europe to complete his studies. He was called to the Palestine Bar in the early 1930s. He also told me that he had been a student at the Sorbonne, the London School of Economics, Speaker's Corner and the University of Brussels, where he had obtained an LLD, a doctorate in laws. Whether he really ever did get this, I don't know, because I have been unable to find out what his thesis was on.

But whether or not he exaggerated his doctorate, he did become a lawyer. I have seen the certificate which said he was a member of the Palestine Bar. He specialised in shipping law, and it was that which brought him, around 1938, to Bucharest, where my mother's family lived.

Her father, Alfred Cappon, was a Romanian mogul and controlled much of the shipping of coal between Romania and the rest of the world. He was so rich he had the first telephone in any bathroom in Bucharest. And it was gold-plated. Alone in his bathroom, my grandfather talked on that epoch-making telephone to his many mistresses.

Alfred's wife couldn't bear to eavesdrop, so she paid one of their maids to listen in on an extension and then report back to her on the endlessly shocking infidelities of her husband. Apparently the eavesdropping maid also went a few rounds in the bedlinen with Alfred, but my grandmother never found out.

According to my father, my mother knew that Alfred was Bucharest's No. 1 philanderer. But Dolly forgave her father.

She forgave him everything. (My mother's three sisters complained that she was spoilt rotten because she was the youngest child. My father agreed entirely.) There is a touching picture of my mother leaning her head on her father's shoulder. She is the adoring and adored daughter. Her mother looks on sternly. Freud would have had a lot to say about that picture, I suspect.

Despite – or perhaps because of – the gold telephone and the mistresses, Alfred was progressive about the education of children. His two youngest daughters got degrees. My Aunt Laura became a doctor and my mother became a lawyer. She was even allowed to ride a motorbike in the Sahara desert with a young man. This seemed an extraordinary expedition for the 1930s. It would be years before I found out who her companion was.

Typically, my parents could not agree on how they courted and why they married in 1939. My mother said it was a mistake: her sister, Laura, bet her that she couldn't seduce the young lawyer from Palestine. My father said they threw her at him because he had a British passport that would save the family from the Nazis.

As I rummaged among their papers, I found a picture of the two of them which suggests that something less cynical was also going on. She is in her late twenties, he is a few years older; they are walking in a park in Bucharest. My father is admiring my mother. He is making a sweeping gesture with his hands. It's almost a ballet dancer's gesture. The sweep, the smile, say, 'Look at you, lady. Look at how beautiful you are.' A lawyer selling it to the jury. My mother smiles, pleased, enjoying the compliment.

I never saw them look so happy again.

The marriage should have worked. They had a lot in common. They were intelligent, they were both lawyers, and they shared a passion for French literature. They both loved good food and the theatre. They could talk about Shakespeare and Racine, Corneille and Goethe. Both liked the traditions of Judaism but neither of them was orthodox in any narrow way.

They were married at the British Embassy in Bucharest and went to Israel.

My father went to work for the British Navy as a lawyer and specialised in requisitioning ships. He got all of his wife's family out of Romania and, typically, as he saw it, they weren't grateful. During the war, he was posted to Cairo.

By the time I was born, they weren't happy. My father was bombastic but an optimist. He always expected he would make his fortune again. My mother was pessimistic. Her childhood and youth had been glorious, elegant and carefree. It had been downhill all the way since then. I didn't work out for years that this also meant that, for her, it had been downhill ever since I was born. She loved me but I had cost her dear.

My father would sometimes complain bitterly that my mother had been warped by her family. 'One incident proved that two hundred per cent,' he said, 'and is a perfect example of her failure to be a good wife, popski.'

During the war, my mother had come to visit my father in Cairo. 'I begged her to be honest, not to abuse the trust that was placed in me as a senior officer. I knew what her family were like. But neither her father nor her eldest brother Relly could bear to miss a chance to make a dishonest dinar. They asked her to smuggle gold sovereigns out of Egypt.'

'Your mother was caught very properly, the officers were only doing their job,' my father added. He had to use all his contacts to hush up the scandal and ensure that my mother wasn't arrested. If it hadn't been for the awful incident, he told me, he would not have ended the war just with an OBE for services to the Ministry of War Transport. He would have been knighted. *Sir* Benjamin Cohen. Bank managers would have crumbled before him. They would have been offering him overdrafts on silver platters.

Predictably, my mother didn't see the Cairo tragedy like that. 'He loved Cairo because he had at least three mistresses there and Egyptian women have no shame,' she told me. He exaggerated the incident of the gold, according to her. It was all a misunderstanding. (One of the mysteries about my mother was how often Customs stopped her on suspicion of smuggling jewels.)

When Israel became independent in 1948, we were there. I was even bombed in my pram on Mount Carmel. Three years later, my father gave up his practice as a lawyer and we left the country. We went to live in Paris. My father was always vague about why he left Israel and why he refused to go back after 1955. Sometimes he'd claim that he had grown up with Arab friends in Haifa. He loved the Koran as much as the Torah. He felt utterly divided in his soul, he would say, as Israel fought with the Arabs.

I don't doubt that that was part of the story, but I am sure there was something else too, some scandal he preferred not to risk reigniting. He took his refusal to visit Israel to extremes. He would not even go to Tel Aviv to visit his mother who lived to the age of 103. If she wanted to see her son, Safta had to be flown to Britain where he always made a huge fuss of her. But even when she died, he would not go to Israel for her funeral.

My father was unfathomable in other ways. He accused my mother's family of being degenerates, of being the sort of bourgeois exploiters whom Marxists would love to string up by their Swiss bank accounts. So why did he go into business with them?

The Pasha of Pondicherry, 1951

Sometime in 1951 I went on what was a huge adventure – long-distance flights were hardly routine then. My father had gone ahead to Pondicherry. My mother and I were to join him. It took days. First we flew from Paris to Pakistan. We landed in the middle of the night at Karachi and paused for twenty-four hours. Then we flew to Calcutta where we had to pause again. I have memories of staying in a dark hotel where we had lemons in the bathroom. The last flight of this epic journey turned into one of the scariest experiences of my life.

We took a DC-3 (propellers – no jet engines) from Calcutta to Madras. As we were flying, we hit a ferocious storm. The plane rocked from side to side. My mother was terrified. I was violently sick. I thought my time had come.

But when we finally landed at Madras, Benjamin was there to meet us. He was wearing a white silk suit and a straw hat. He was accompanied by his driver and a young woman in her twenties whom he introduced as his secretary, Miss Kaminjee.

From Madras we drove the hundred-odd kilometres to Pondicherry. The road was magical. At one point in the jungle, the driver stopped to show us a family of elephants standing in a clearing. The reason we went to India was less idyllic. My father and my Uncle Relly had decided to work together. At the time, of course, my father did not complain that Dolly's brother was a 'corrupt entity' and that 'one day the Marxists will string him up'.

Today, Pondicherry is famous because there is a

fashionable ashram there. Now, of course, it is part of India. But in the early 1950s it was still a French colony, and had been for the best part of a century and a half. It was a small and pretty port near the south-eastern tip of India.

We were part of the small European elite that ran the colony. The senior French military and civil servants lived in beautiful French colonial houses. We lived in the best hotel. The hotel only had room for six other guests. Our suite gave on to a large terrace. A huge flapping mosquito net was draped round my bed. It was full of holes and I got bitten all the time.

'They love your blood,' my mother said, 'because it's so sweet.'

It was hard to sleep because of the heat and the bugs. When she put me to bed, my mother would cover me with antiseptic creams and warn me not to scratch. If I scratched, I'd get infected all over. Every morning, my father would order breakfast – bread and boiled eggs. He would sit on the terrace in billowing white trousers and read the *Times of India*. When the boiled eggs came, he'd mash them up with lemon juice and olive oil. It was the best food I'd ever eaten. We seemed to be a happy family.

After breakfast, my father would go to his office. My mother would sunbathe and do her gymnastic exercises. She was an avid believer in physical exercise and could do the splits well into her sixties. After that, she would read. I wasn't allowed to play with the Indian children and, because there were no other European children, I was alone and bored most of the time. The person with whom I spent most time was my mother.

No one explained to me what my father and uncle were doing. I fear the murky truth is something like this (and it's a miracle the Marxists didn't string them both up).

My father would cross the border into India proper. He would buy gold dirt cheap from poor Indians in Madras and the surrounding countryside. He paid them in rupees and rupees were hardly worth the paper they were printed on. My father and uncle would then bring the gold back across the pretty non-existent border. From Pondicherry, the gold would be shipped back to Europe where my uncle would sell it at the market price of $38 an ounce. The profits were huge.

The Indian government was powerless to stop the exploitation but it made endless diplomatic protests to the French. Every so often, to pacify Delhi, my father would be arrested by the Préfet de Police, Monsieur Le Roi ('Mr King' in English). I liked Monsieur Le Roi.

I kept asking him, 'Mr King, where is your crown?'

Monsieur Le Roi would go beetroot with laughter. He would mime putting a crown on his head. 'Now I'm a king,' he'd laugh.

My mother would always laugh too. My father would tell her later that it had been stupid of her to spoil me by making so much of my very silly joke.

Officially, the French government did not approve of smuggling; unofficially, the French turned a blind eye. I suspect now that many French and Indian officials were being paid bribes to let the gold through. But, as I say, to show the Indians that the French did not tolerate criminal activities, my father would be arrested regularly. I never knew that was happening, however. Monsieur Le Roi didn't want to upset me by dragging my father off in handcuffs. So I was told that he and my father were leaving the hotel to go and have coffee.

A hundred yards from the hotel Monsieur Le Roi would hand him over to the police. Telegrams would be sent to

Delhi announcing a triumph for the forces of law and order. The French had arrested the wicked smuggler Cohen. He was languishing in Pondicherry Prison, which was worse than the Black Hole of Calcutta.

An hour or so later, Monsieur Le Roi would come down to the cells and tell the guards to go. He had to interrogate the evil Cohen in person. When they were alone, Le Roi would bring out a bottle of champagne and they would play backgammon into the early hours.

After twenty-four hours, the evidence against Cohen would turn out to be flawed. Witnesses had changed their story. Some had fled to Ceylon; others were last seen jumping onto an elephant and galloping into the jungle. French laws were based on the Code Napoleon. You could not hold a man just because he might have done something. Cohen was innocent till proven guilty. To the immense regret of the French authorities, the probably wicked but not-yet-nailed smuggler Cohen had to be released.

How much money was required for French officials to turn a blind eye, I never found out. But I'm sure they did fine out of it.

My father didn't just diddle the Indians; as far as he was concerned, he was bringing them art and literature. He saw himself as a pasha of culture. He brought a large number of reproductions of Impressionist paintings from Paris and set up a museum. Free of charge, Indians could admire copies of Van Gogh and Monet. My father typed out little explanations of the pictures and short biographies of the artists to help the locals understand the wonders of Western culture. He was very pleased that many of the inhabitants visited it often.

My father was nearly always in a good mood in Pondicherry. So was my mother but for different reasons. She did her best to avoid all the locals, but she had time and servants. She was a worshipper of the body beautiful. She spent hours sunbathing on the veranda or doing her gymnastic exercises.

And then ... I put my foot smack in the idyll.

My father's office was 200 yards from the hotel. My mother was siesta-ing on the veranda. I was bored. My father would be pleased to see me, I thought. I tiptoed down the stairs past the one-eared stuffed tiger, the only item of interest in the hotel lobby.

Pondicherry was dozing in the afternoon sun. Mosquitoes were taking a well-earned siesta too; they had to be rested to bite us so enthusiastically during the night.

I walked over to my father's office. I wasn't trying to be quiet. I opened the door and said, 'I thought I'd come to see you, Papa.'

Benjamin Cohen OBE, however, was stark naked.

'Didn't your mother teach you to knock,' my father yelled. He jumped up from the chaise longue to reveal another naked body below his.

Miss Kaminjee, his secretary, screamed. She was naked. I was rooted to the spot. I'd never even seen my mother naked. Miss Kaminjee's breasts stood out, taut, round and brown like big scoops of coffee ice cream. She scrabbled to find her sari, but it had fallen down the side of the chaise longue. She flustered on to the floor.

'Get out,' my father shouted.

Unable to retrieve her sari, Miss Kaminjee grabbed a copy of the *Times of India* and covered as much of her nakedness as she could with its pages.

'Get out, *peseveke*,' my father yelled. *Peseveke* was an Arab word of infinite badness. Then, still naked, he punched me hard, pushed me out of the door and slammed it behind me.

I was terrified. Inside he continued shouting abuse at

me. I ran back to the hotel. My mother was still sleeping on
the veranda.

I was crying. I knew my mother would be annoyed if I
woke her. I didn't know what to do. Then, I made the fatal
mistake. I shook my mother awake.

'What's the matter?' she said.

'Papa hit me,' I cried.

'Why?'

'He's naked.'

'Naked?' She was, all of a sudden, alert. She could sniff
out infidelity at fifty paces. 'Naked in the office?' She spoke
calmly, slowly. 'And is anyone else naked in the office too?'

I must have blushed.

'I asked you a question, David. Is anyone else naked in
his so-called office?'

But she already knew the answer. She got up, grabbed
my hand and marched me down the stairs past the tiger
again. I sobbed that I didn't want to go.

By the time we reached the office, my father was fully
dressed. He was dictating to a demurely sari-ed Miss
Kaminjee.

'The shipment you will receive—am I going too fast,
Miss Kaminjee?' He stopped and smiled. 'Ah, my good wife,
what a nice surprise.'

'Don't insult me,' my mother said, 'Casanova.'

'We are working here, trying to gain an economic crust.'

'Leave me with my husband,' my mother said to Miss
Kaminjee. Miss Kaminjee looked to my father for protection
and instructions. 'Get out, you slut,' my mother shouted.
Miss Kaminjee turned and fled.

'So now you go with brown women. Have you no shame?'

'You're mad. I've no idea what you think was going on
here.'

'David, did you see your father naked with Miss Kaminjee?'
I burst into tears.

'So you want to use the child as a witness against the father,' my father yelled. 'You Romanians have no ethics. If you say a word, David, I will be eternally ashamed of you.'

'You want your son to lie for you,' my mother countered, 'very ethical. Which rabbi recommends it?'

I couldn't stop crying.

'You see what you've done to the child,' my mother went on. 'Why couldn't you even lock the door?' She could be extremely practical.

'I have work to do. Leave me in peace.'

My mother said she would leave him in peace indeed. She would leave India with its diseases, beggars, bugs and brown sirens. Benjamin could stay behind for so-called business, dirty business, monkey business, but she was not going to risk cholera and beriberi while he took his clothes off with strange women.

The week before my mother and I left was not spent in awkward silence. My parents specialised in slanging matches and majored in 'I have suffered more than you' performances. She complained that she had sacrificed so much for him, had come out to India, which she hated, and even eaten curries. She had risked her health and my health. He boasted of his even greater sacrifices. She had ruined his career. He brought up her attempt to smuggle gold in Egypt. She had never been a good wife to him. When he said that, he sometimes flew into one of his rages, going red in the face. His eyes would bulge. The sheer energy of his fury was frightening. And, he said, she knew the other thing, which he had promised never to mention in front of me, so he wasn't mentioning it. But she knew what he meant.

At that my mother would grab me and walk out.

'Your father gets too angry. My father was never angry like that,' she would say.

My mother and I flew back to Israel and went to live in a big house halfway up Mount Carmel.

Nine months after we left him, my father reappeared in Israel. He persuaded my mother that they should make a fresh start in a fresh country.

'Let us bury Miss Kaminjee,' he said.

'I will agree,' said my mother, 'for the good of our son'.

('I asked him how many Miss Kaminjees there were but, of course, I didn't get an answer,' my mother said later.)

Our newly reunited family went to Geneva. We were very rich thanks to my father and Uncle Relly's having diddled the poor Indian masses out of their gold. We put up in the very grand Hotel du Rhône – and in a small suite. King Farouk of Egypt had a suite on the same floor.

It was there we heard on the radio of the death of Stalin.

My mother was delighted.

After a few months, however, we were no longer rich. We had to move out of the grand hotel. 'Your father is good at making money and good at losing money,' my mother sighed. I was sent to the Ecole International where the classes were in English. For the first time in my life, I made some friends of my own age. I started to collect Meccano and Dinky toys. I was not as happy as I'd been in Pondicherry – I didn't realise that it was because I was seeing less of my mother – but happy enough.

There was one panic which shows how violent my father could get. I was in a park playing with my ball when another small boy tried to swipe it. I grabbed it back.

'What's your name?' his angry father demanded.

'David Cohen,' I said.

'Filthy Jew,' he shouted.

I ran home crying. My mother calmed me down. But when my father came back a little later, he went berserk. He shouted was going to teach the anti-Semites a lesson. My mother begged him not to do anything rash. We would get in trouble with the police.

But he wasn't listening.

'We'll find the bastard and teach him a lesson he won't forget,' Benjamin Cohen OBE insisted.

We scoured the park for the anti-Semite but, probably for the best, we didn't find him.

A few months later, my father returned to our small flat in a tragic mood. The anti-Semitic Swiss had refused to renew his work permit.

We were being thrown out of Switzerland. I discovered years later that my father's business partner, my Uncle Relly, had been caught trying to sell fake krugerrands in Switzerland. He fled back to Israel on a diplomatic passport. I don't suppose that made the Swiss more disposed to let us stay. They may have done some extra checks and discovered that my uncle Zoli was also smuggling in Switzerland. He had wanted to be a poet but it is hard to earn your daily salami by writing sonnets in Hungarian, so he became a money smuggler instead. As you do.

When I think about the choice my father made when the Swiss kicked us out, I'm baffled. I never understood why he didn't return to Israel. He had friends, family and good connections there. He had lost the Pondicherry millions but he still had a good deal of money. He could practise law, he could even go into politics. Many people there admired him. My mother loved Israel and was keen to return. Instead, he decided to head for London, a city where neither of my parents knew a soul. I realised much later why he had made this decision. It was the strange faith colonials often had in the fairness of Britain. After all, he had a British passport and an OBE.

Today, teachers and social workers are aware of the problems children face when they come to live in a new country. In the 1950s, we just arrived here and I had to get on with it.

We booked into the Stratford Court Hotel off Oxford Street. The first morning my father took me on a double-decker bus to see London. He was very jovial, and I liked the fact that he was showing me the city, but it still seemed so very strange to be here – and so suddenly.

Over breakfast, my father handed me *The Times*. It was important to find out about our new country. I was a football fan and I turned to the sports pages. I was annoyed there were no reports about my favourite French or Swiss football teams but I was struck by a very peculiar set of sports results. I could understand the football scores but what was the meaning of:

Bedser ct Brown b Titmus 1

What did 'ht.wkt' mean or 'b' or 'ct Edrich b'?

I promised myself that I would learn what this strange language meant and how cricket was played.

Most Jews, when they come to a new country, head for the synagogue. My mother started going to the Reform Synagogue in Upper Berkeley Street. It is a very grand place of worship and is the home of Reform Judaism. But my father made fun of it. If you were going to go to synagogue, you should go to real one, not one where half the service was in English. Worse, the rabbi spoke Hebrew with a ridiculous Dutch South African accent. This wasn't the way Moses spoke, my father told my mother.

'God speaks in many languages. I believe it is not possible to be devout without understanding the Koran as well as the Torah. I suggest you learn Arabic,' my father said to the rabbi, Dr van der Zyl.

My mother apologised in German. Her husband was a barbarian. He only liked the Koran because it allowed men to have four wives and a harem.

My father said it was unfortunate that my mother had no religious culture, but since the rabbi hadn't read the Koran, he wouldn't know or care.

My mother complained that my father had been so rude to the rabbi she could hardly show her face at the synagogue. She went there to pray but never joined in the social activities.

'This rabbi is a narrow minded Pharisee,' my father declared – and he would have no truck with bloody Pharisees. He was being unjust to van der Zyl, who was a clever and, indeed, good man.

We lodged at first with a Mrs Popham, whose husband, I believed, had been an Indian civil servant, and her house in Kensington was half a museum. I have subsequently found out that she was the widow of Edward Popham, who had been one of the British civil servants who ran Palestine when it was under the Mandate in the 1930s.

My parents had very little idea what to do with me. In Israel I had been to the Reali School, one of the oldest private schools in Israel; in Geneva I went to the International School, whose head teacher was delighted to note that I no longer expressed myself in French. My father had a rather romantic notion of how excellent English schools were.

My mother was in a foreign city and very lonely. She took me on expeditions sometimes to explore the only area in London that felt a little familiar, Soho. She could buy tournedos at the French butcher, Randall and Aubin, and chat in French with the fat lady who owned it. She could have proper coffee and cakes at Patisserie Valerie in Old Compton Street. She could discuss the different salamis available at the Italian grocers Camisa's on the same street.

She loved Soho. She breezed past doorways which offered Delicious Dames and Gorgeous Models upstairs and said she had seen far more brazen things in Cairo and India.

Men were always men, she sniped.

I loved these expeditions with her. I felt so close to her. She often took my arm. She was in her late forties, pretty and fit as a fiddle. Sometimes, as we had cakes at Valerie's or milk shakes at Fortnum and Mason, she'd pick the moment to warn me. My father always exaggerated money problems. He didn't want her to have pretty dresses or enjoy herself. He was unjust saying that her family had not just spoiled her but warped her. She'd never done an honest day's work in her life, she'd never earned a penny by the sweat of her brow and, therefore, she had no idea of the value of money.

These tensions erupted when my parents had to decide where to live. My mother wanted to buy a house because that was sensible and paying rent was just money wasted. My father pointed out that this was typical of her unrealistic attitude. They did not have the money to buy a house. Needless to say that did not stop my mother visiting estate agents in the hope of finding such a wonderful deal my father would change his mind. She was especially keen on a pink house with bow windows opposite Regent's Park. I have no idea how much it cost but I suspect it was not cheap. My father refused to even look at it.

In the end my father won, and they rented a flat in a new red-brick block in Seymour Place near Marble Arch. At the back there was a small mews and a wall, behind which there was a huge bomb site. Wild plants grew in profusion – it was a great place to explore. Opposite the flat in Seymour

Place there was a Christian Scientist church. Today the whole area is Arabia Minor but at the end of the 1950s it was staunchly English and very middle class. My mother liked one thing about it. There was a good swimming pool, Seymour Baths, two minutes away.

Our flat was on the ground floor. It had a living room, a dining room and two bedrooms. The kitchen was tiny and had a miniscule balcony which looked down on the mews at the rear. The flat was quite small and had all the character of a blank piece of paper. We rented unfurnished. How to furnish it provoked yet another quarrel. My father said we could only afford something very basic, but my mother wanted a smart leather sofa from Harrods and, eventually, nagged him so much he bought it on H.P. The walls of the flat were so thin so that you could hear everything. At night, lying in bed, I could hear my parents quarrel. Quarrel in French, quarrel in English. He'd often swear at her in Hebrew and Arabic. The subjects were usually the same. His unfaithfulness. Her extravagance. Her family and how had it ruined, corrupted and warped her.

My parents even quarrelled about sport. As I have said, my mother was a keep-fit fanatic and spent at least an hour a day doing gymnastic exercises. My father thought this was stupid and only showed how vain she was. So he was not at all impressed when I discovered I was good at 'games'.

Israel was another cause of dissent. Ironically, though Benjamin had been born in Israel, my mother was far more interested in the country than he was. She adored it. They could still go back, she insisted. She couldn't see the point of living here in London. The weather was lousy. They had no friends. But, as I say, he had no intention of ever going back – and he never really explained why. It was a mystery he took to the grave with him.

I hated the rows. And they were often worst when I was put to bed.

I felt I had to find some way to stop them arguing.

'Goodnight, sleep well,' I'd call to them from my room.

One of them always replied, 'Goodnight.'

Then, without stopping for breath, they'd start shouting at each other again.

I'd say goodnight again.

'I heard you. Goodnight, sleep well,' my father would say.

Then they would start again, hammer and tongs.

Children feel they are to blame when their parents are unhappy and even more so when they divorce, according to at least fifty studies of the effects of divorce. It must be something the child did or did not do that made their parents split up, or at least so the child thinks. I don't remember feeling that kind of guilt. What I did feel was that I should make it better for them – and for myself.

It took a death to make them feel tenderness for each other. When my mother's mother died on the 19th of February 1957, my father embraced my mother in his office while she cried and cried. We went to the synagogue and this time he did not denounce the rabbi. My father told me I had to be especially kind to my mother. 'But I know I can rely on you to be a gentleman, popski.'

It was the last time I ever saw them embrace or even be nice to each other.

The Glories of English Education
In the late 1950s, London was not the multicultural metropolis it is today. My parents had to find me a school, and the trouble was, I was at an awkward age. I was nine years old, too young to sit the eleven-plus and far too young to go to public school.

My mother wrote to my old school in Geneva and asked for advice. The headmistress of the Ecole Internationale said that, as I was bright, I should go to Colet Court, the preparatory school for St Paul's, which would, in turn, prepare me for Oxbridge.

I was too old for 'normal' entry to Colet Court, but since my father had an OBE, the headmaster was willing to see us. My mother fluttered her eyelashes at him, while my father dropped names of admirals he had worked for. The headmaster was not impressed. He asked me a few questions and shook his head as it became clear that I had never done any Latin and knew nothing about the kings and queens of England. Schools in France, Switzerland or Israel should be ashamed of themselves for not teaching English history. A boy of my age should be able to reel off why King John was bad and why Queen Elizabeth was great.

I was not exceptional, the headmaster said. He might have been willing to admit an exceptional boy. But I did not cut the mustard.

My parents were desperately upset. I had a string of good school reports. My father promised he would make the headmaster eat his mortarboard.

Things were not going too well with the neighbours in Vincent Court either. Just above us lived Mrs Olson, who was enormously fat – she ran a snack bar in Mayfair – and her two equally fat children. Jill, her daughter, was in her early twenties and Richard was my own age. He was a bully and I was the perfect butt for him because I did not know the rules of my new land.

Richard loved a game called Double or Quits. He insisted I play it with him. I didn't dare refuse because I wanted to be accepted. I didn't dare admit either that I never understood the rules as he described them. I could never quit –

and never win. Often, at the end of an hour's play, I was seething with frustration while Richard grinned in podgy ecstasy. I never discovered how to play Double or Quits and so I did my best to avoid him. That offended his mother, who had somehow gathered from my mother that no school had accepted me. Eager to show how foreigners needed help, Mrs Olson suggested that my parents go to talk to Eaton House near Sloane Square – Richard's school. I dreaded, of course, going to the same school as my tormentor. But it was the end of the summer and I had to be educated somewhere.

Eaton House was less fussy than any other school that my parents approached. If you could read, write and your parents could pay the fees, you were good enough for them. The school had been set up by some relative of Gladstone, and Gladstone would have been appalled by what was being done in his name sixty years after his death.

In the late 1950s, Eaton House was under the impression that the Second World War had not ended. Many masters liked to be known by their military ranks. Colonel Barrow taught maths, and Major Hyams was responsible for Latin and Greek. (I have changed the names to protect the guilty.) Major Holberton, long-faced and with the look of Don Quixote, was one of the two headmasters. One of the few teachers who did not parade his rank was Mr Lemon, who looked like a beetroot and was the other headmaster. It was typical of the eccentricity of Eaton House that it should have two headmasters. The reason was that Mr Lemon owned the place but the only subject he knew much about was whisky. He often smelled of it.

Fees were £32 a term and you paid extra for football, cricket and piano. My father filed away many papers relating to my schooldays, so I know the charges. As well as my school uniform, I had to have a football hose (price £1) and twelve handkerchiefs. It was against school rules to wipe your snot on your sleeve.

Some of the school rules were decidedly eccentric – and some seemed to me to have been devised to give masters every chance to beat boys. With hindsight I have no doubt that some of the masters were sadists (and one, I discovered later, was deeply troubled because his wife had slept with most of the toffs in Eaton Square).

In Israel and in Switzerland, I had never been beaten at school. In London I was terrified to discover it happened all the time. There were at least three kinds of beatings – the least serious was the slipper and the most serious was the cane. In between there was the Jokari paddle, a sort of small wooden tennis racquet which, in its more innocent guise, was attached by a piece of elastic to a rubber ball. The Latin master beat the boys with this for a variety of reasons.

If we got our Latin declensions wrong – to teach us Latin.

If we were late – to teach us punctuality.

If we spoke too little in class – to cure shyness.

If we spoke too much in class – to stop us thinking we were interesting.

If we got our Latin declensions right – to teach us humility.

If we looked scared – to teach us courage.

If we looked untidy – to teach us not to look untidy.

And the utterly incomprehensible rule: If the Latin master suspected our mothers had tied our shoelaces.

Colonel Barrow, maths, liked to flick lighted matches at us. He was an optimist and told us straight that he hoped one day to set fire to a boy's hair.

But it was not just the staff who were bizarre. The boys played a game I'd never played in any of my other schools.

You placed the school cap over your genitals. Like two fencers, you then circled each other. Then you flicked your cap in the general direction of the other's boy genitals. If you scored a hit, you were allowed to cry 'Balls'. In theory, the masters disapproved of this game. In practice, they often watched and, occasionally, took part in it. We all understood we were never to play this game in front of the wife of either headmaster.

There was one rebel on the staff, the English master, John Buckland. He refused to use a cane because it was inhuman. He sported a handlebar moustache, smoked Park Drives right down to the butt and was a composer in his spare time. His triumph was that he had composed the music for a production of *Coriolanus* on the *Third Programme*. He nicknamed me 'Heffalump'. I had not read the Winnie the Pooh stories so I had no idea what a heffalump might be, but I knew Buckland was making fun of me. It upset me to be ridiculed and upset me even more that I did not quite know how I was being ridiculed.

When I asked my parents what a heffalump was, they had no idea either.

But while the culture around me was often baffling, the textbooks were easy. It was not hard to learn the dates of the kings and queens of England, and why King John had been so bad and Queen Elizabeth so glorious. Within a year my reports said what my father had expected them to say – I was top of the class. Some of the credit was due to Mr Buckland, but I later found out – as I read through my father's letters – that he was bribing Buckland. He offered Buckland small loans and paid him – in theory – for extra tuition but which really meant that Buckland would pay special attention to me. To my father baksheesh was a way of life, and I think it rather pleased him to give the respectable

English – those paragons of fair play – a little baksheesh.

From time to time, I went to visit Mr Buckland at his house in far-off New Cross so that he could give me extra lessons. I needed them, Buckland told my father. In his informal reports, he complained of my appalling hand-writing and my sloppy mistakes. I was clever but careless. Still, I was making good progress, and he did not think there was reason for serious concern. Buckland obviously had real money problems. Before Christmas 1957, he wrote to my father, 'I would be grateful if I may be paid in cash.' My father, being a lawyer, kept all the evidence.

In the report Buckland wrote to my father at the end of 1957, he noted, 'I know of no technique where one can erad-icate errors since adults often do the same.' He could only hope I would grow out of it. Buckland consoled my father because his own son, who had won a place at the City of London grammar school, also committed 'the same sort of grotesque and ridiculous mistakes. By continuing to pull David up when he does I think one is doing all that is possible.'

My father was not best pleased with this letter and yelled at me that I was not trying. I became very fearful when he was in one of these moods, and with good reason. My father was often violent. He loomed over me, grabbed me by the shoulder and slapped me three times.

My mother burst into tears.

'Do you want to make him a baby,' my red-faced father screamed. He slapped me another three times very hard on the face.

'You'll be a nothing, a *vaux rien*,' my father added. *Vaux rien* is French for 'worth nothing'. He pushed me away.

When he yelled that he had wasted his time, energy and money on me, I was in tears.

'If you don't stop crying, I'll slap you again,' he yelled.

My mother was rarely able to calm him down. After he had hit me, he told me to go to my room and think about why I made so many mistakes.

This particular beating seemed so harsh to me because I was doing well at school. Quite apart from school work, I had good hand-eye co-ordination and so I became the goal-keeper of the school football team. I even mastered the mysteries of cricket and opened the batting for the school. My father thought, however, that cricket and football could only interfere with serious work.

He was not surprised therefore when the headmaster, Major Holberton, wrote to say that my father had to visit the school to discuss something confidential.

'If you've done something wrong, tell me. Tell me now, and always tell the truth,' my father yelled.

I hadn't done anything, I pleaded.

'It's better if I know now,' my father glowered.

But I really couldn't think of anything I'd done wrong.

'I hope I don't find out my son is a liar.'

I thought he was going to beat me again. He tended to hit me more when his business was going badly and recently he had been complaining about the stock market.

But he steadied himself, poured himself a cognac and left.

My mother and I waited anxiously for him to return. He came back looking pensive.

'What happened?' I asked.

'Do you think you're in trouble, do you think I'm going to punish you?'

His words made me tense up. I sensed another beating on the way. He didn't wait long before he burst out laughing and told me I had nothing to worry about. The meeting had gone like this ...

Dr Benjamin Cohen OBE enters the study of Major

Holberton. Holberton is embarrassed. He says my father may sit down. Holberton starts on a potted history of the school, which is over sixty years old.

My father becomes more anxious. Clearly this speech has only one conclusion. I am sorry to say, Dr Cohen, that your son is not fit to be in this high-class English institution.

Holberton sighs. He looks very ill at ease. Then he says, 'I better come to the point. It's a damn shame for a school like ours to have to have a Jewboy as its head boy.'

My father is not sure he has heard right. Gingerly, he asks, 'My son isn't up the creek, as they used to say in the navy, Major?'

'No, the school's up the creek. We wouldn't make a Jewboy head boy if we could possibly avoid it. Thank God half the boys in the school aren't British.'

That was all right then. A yid could lord it over the wogs, blackies, nig-nogs, chinks, dagoes and eyeties.

My father finally grasped the situation. I had become one of the officer class. 'I'm very grateful,' he said and shook the Major's hand. If he'd had a cap, he'd have doffed it. The English gents were making his son head boy. Never mind if they thought it was a shame – for him, it was a triumph.

'He was a gentleman about it,' my father told us, and he bought champagne to celebrate.

I hoped that my being made head boy would make my parents happier. But it didn't, and, contrary to expectations, it made me rather unhappy. I had no idea what you had to do to be a good head boy in this strange country. For that and many other reasons, I was becoming terribly anxious.

Separation Anxiety
According to Freud, to know the root of your anxieties is to start curing yourself of them. If I had never been so

desperately anxious before, at least I understood what was making me anxious now. But knowing didn't help.

I was terrified that my mother would not be home when I got back from school. I suppose a shrink would balloon this up into a dread that she would disappear completely.

I'd set off home from Sloane Square on the 137 bus. As I walked from Marble Arch towards Vincent Court, I started to look for omens. If the two men in the mews garage behind the flats were mending cars, that was a good omen. She'd be there.

If a car was parked outside Vincent Court and the letters on the number plate made up a word or a syllable like VUT, that was also a good omen. She'd be there.

When I got to the entrance of Vincent Court, I'd agonise. Should I ring the bell or use my own key? If I rang, I might be lucky and get an immediate answer. Panic over. But if I rang and there was no answer? Total panic.

If I rang and there was no answer, I counted to twelve, then to eighteen – she could be in the bathroom after all. But by the time I'd reached twenty-four, there was no disguising the truth. She was out.

If I used the key, I dreaded the moment I opened the door and shouted 'Maman'. I dreaded silence, finding out that she wasn't there.

If she weren't there, I hated having to wait for her. I'd be listening for every footstep, hoping it would be hers.

I developed rituals to cope. I'd close my eyes and count to a hundred. If that hadn't magicked her home, I'd walk around the block. Every step needed a decision. First, should I turn right or left outside the entrance?

Then, which way to go? South towards Marble Arch? West towards the Edgware Road?

I often chose the route that she was likely to take. Then I

might meet her and, if I did, I had enough sense to act casual. I always had a good explanation ready, as I didn't want her to know I was looking for her. I'd gone out because I wanted Rowntree's fruit gums, or a pencil, or the *Evening Standard*. But I never went too far. I always had to come back to the flat within ten to fifteen minutes to check if she'd come back while I was out.

Sometimes, cunning pre-teen, I walked a way I knew she'd never take. She never walked north, to the far end of Seymour Place where the Seymour Baths were. If I went north, I couldn't be disappointed not to find her. There was less than a one in a hundred chance I'd meet her.

Once she did not turn up for three hours. She hadn't left me a note. I was so beside myself that I walked to the block of flats where her best friend Mrs Amram lived. I didn't dare go up. So I loitered in the lobby, and when the porter asked me whom I wanted, I ran out.

As we shall see, I still hate waiting. It causes more problems than you might imagine.

Children Shouldn't Know About Sex

My parents did not suffer their unhappiness in silence. They were always offering the evidence which proved that their spouse had done them wrong. They carped, complained, accused, ranted. And, as their only child, I was often a jury of one.

'Of course, a mother has the right to expect her son to love her and be loyal, but of course your father talks so well, he could talk the trunk off the elephants.' One of the books she read me was Babar the elephant stories.

'Of course, popski, a son must always be loyal to his mother, but let me put the facts of the case in front of you, as a rational man …'

I was nine at the time.

And while, thanks to my father, I became more rational, thanks to my mother, I became less innocent. Sometimes when I got home and, miraculously, my mother was in, she would be hosting a tea party for two or three friends. In German and Romanian (which they all forgot I understood) they discussed their husbands. One of my mother's friends had been the lover of her father, Alfred. These elegant, cynical women sighed at the fate of the female sex. Unfaithful husbands, deceivers ever, were always ready to fritter money on some dumb blonde, money which could have been spent on diamonds for a good wife or at the very least on some fine furniture.

In the wake of the pants-down-in-Pondicherry farce, one of my mother's saddest jokes was that her husband didn't have secretaries but sex-retaries. Secretaries were the enemy. If men were after just one thing (which secretaries had in spades), secretaries were only after one thing too – and that was marriage. Even if it meant getting your boss to divorce his loyal, long-suffering wife.

By the time I was nine, my mother had made it plain to me. 'Your father is a Casanova. But then you know he was a Casanova in India.' I was, of course, expected to know who Casanova was and the kind of things he got up to.

The cynical ladies and the talk of Casanova was not very personal. It was a third event made me lose my innocence in a far more dramatic way. In Geneva, my father had hired Evi to work for him. My mother very quickly nosed out that she was a threat. Evi was Jewish and well educated. She was not beautiful but she was rich. She admired and adored my father, who was some fifteen years older than her. When Evi followed us to London to help my father set up his office, my mother became convinced. Evi was after my father.

Rather strangely, my father agreed. Yes, Evi was infatuated with him but she was a '*pauvre fille*'. She had lost her father, some man had jilted her. She wanted guidance and my father felt that it was his moral duty to provide it. Did not the Talmud say 'and when the maidservant is distressed, it is thy duty as her master to assist her'?

For 'maidservant' you could read 'secretary', and for 'master' the boss who, like all bosses, my mother said, was looking for any excuse to remove his trousers.

'*La pauvre fille*', my father agreed, needed a husband. And my mother would have to help her find one. They were unusually united in this. They put on their best manners and invited a number of bachelors to dinner. The dinners usually ended in catastrophe.

In the summer of 1957, my mother, Evi and I went on holiday again. I would write to my father with accounts of with the latest details of my swimming and the beaux they were trying to persuade to marry Evi. A certain Mr Isaacstein looked like a 'real possibility'. But something went wrong. Often I wrote to my father that I missed him, that I hoped he wasn't too exhausted and that he would join us. That seemed less likely when we sailed (somehow my mother got us upgraded to first class) from Marseilles to Haifa.

As soon as we landed, my mother resumed her mission to find a husband for Evi. She seemed to be in luck. My father had a cousin called Jacques who was a lawyer and bore an uncanny similarity to Gene Kelly. He liked Evi and for a few weeks all went well. Evi looked radiant. He often called for her.

Then one day Jacques, due to meet Evi for dinner, had to cancel. The Arab cleaning lady took the message, which explained that a case in Jerusalem was going to last an extra day. Just like my mother, Evi thought all Arabs were liars.

She didn't believe Jacques had cancelled their date. The cleaning lady said she had jotted down the message on a scrap of paper. I helped Evi search all over the house to find this jotting. She became more and more angry when she couldn't find the note. The obvious answer was that the paper had been thrown away.

But Evi wouldn't let it rest. She went into the garden to see if the scrap of paper had been thrown away there. My mother begged her to stop but Evi couldn't. When Jacques found out about the incident with the dustbin, he became very cool. They never married.

We came back to London. My mother thought she was safe. My father would also have been warned what Evi was really like. And then, one day, unannounced, Evi pressed the doorbell at Vincent Court.

Evi informed my mother that she had to speak to her even though they were friends. She loved Benjamin. She wanted him, she would have children by him.

They both screamed at each other. After Evi had left, my mother cried. She made herself up again and told me, 'When your father comes home tonight, ask him about his mistress.'

'Maman ...' I said.

'Ask him, if you're really my son and you love your mother,' my mother said.

When my father arrived home, my mother refused to speak to him. She darted meaningful looks at me. I was too scared to open my mouth.

'David has a question to ask you,' she said finally.

'Well, popski, what do you want to ask?'

I couldn't speak. I looked down at my feet. I was sure I was about to be beaten to within an inch of my life by my father. My mother glared at me. Was I, her only son, going to disappoint her.

'Maman asked me to ask you if Evi is really your mistress?'

'Always look a man in the eyes when you ask him a question,' my father replied coolly. The empire-wallahs had curried him in their clichés. Wait till you see the whites of their eyes before you gun them down.

'You see, he doesn't answer the question,' my mother pointed out to me, the jury. 'Ask him about the disgusting things I find in his pockets,' she added for the benefit of the nine-year-old jury. The 'disgusting things' were the Durex. I didn't have the slightest idea what these were, of course, though they did sound Latin. Durex, Durexes, Dureximus.

My father laughed at my mother. It was the Electra complex again. Her father had been unfaithful, so all men had to be unfaithful. Evi was a *pauvre fille* who had her fantasies. No sane person, my father insisted, would call round to make the kind of scene my mother was describing, so either my mother was exaggerating (as usual) or Evi was '*pas bien dans la tête*' – not right in the head. If it would make my mother happier, he would only see Evi in the office.

'We know what people do in offices,' my mother said, invoking Miss Kaminjee.

They patched up a marital peace but my mother believed my father less and less. My father, in turn, had not been doing well. He had lost some money on oil shares, which made him literally hopping mad. If you haven't seen a man hopping mad once in your life, you should. He danced like a dervish in his long johns round the living room, screaming curses at the crooks of BP and Shell.

'I thought someone was being murdered,' Upstairs said as she knocked on the door. Mrs Olson was always pointing out that we didn't know how decent people should behave and threatening to call the police to stop the foreigners murdering each other.

'I'll murder you,' my father yelled and slammed the door in her face.

In deep crisis because of the oil shares, my father wrote an agreement under which Evi would loan him £20,000, a fantastic sum in 1957. It was to be repaid at £10 a week for seven years. In 1970, by means of some unspecified miracle, the balance of some £16,000 still owing would then be repaid. My mother was meant to sign it and a rider, which promised never to deny the debt or challenge the terms of the loan.

But Benjamin Cohen OBE soon had another idea which would get him out of the oil jam. And I didn't realise how devious it was until I was much older. After all, he was my father.

Casanova would have been proud of him.

Chapter 2

Home Alone 1958

In 1958 there was a drama at my prep school. The Major was found hanging in his office. Apparently, he had apparently been having an affair with the secretary. When my mother heard of this it only confirmed her dim view of secretaries. The tragedy scuppered any chance of Prince Charles coming to Eaton House as a pupil.

If the Major had not committed suicide – which my father pointed out was a sin according to every major religion – he would have been able to claim some credit for a great triumph. After having been humiliated at Colet Court, my father was determined I should get into St Paul's. I spent weeks before the exam swotting. Mr Buckland spent many hours teaching me how to write better English. After the Major's death, Mr Lemon hired a new headmaster, Mr de la Condamine, who liked me and gave me extra Latin.

I went off to sit the St Paul's scholarship exam as well prepared as any child could be. One of the problems immigrant children face is that they lack confidence, but Eaton House had given me that. I knew I was clever. I wrote a smarty-pants essay on bad King John in which I argued King John was not bad at all since he had set up the civil service, which was certainly forward-looking of him. I was, of course, merely parroting a book by a historian called Warren, but you had to be a pretty smart twelve-year-old to discover that such a book existed and then to reproduce its arguments.

After the exam I was interviewed by two terrifying masters. One of them was a legend in the public schools at the time. Mr Whitty wore a beret and was famous as a numismatist. He knew perfectly well where I'd got my ideas on King John, and he grilled me to make sure I didn't get too big for my intellectual boots.

But I did it. I became a scholar of St Paul's.

My father took us to celebrate at the Ecu de France, but the celebration didn't last very long. By the time the main course was served, my father was in one of his cataclysmic moods.

'I don't see how I can pay for you to go to St Paul's, sadly,' he said. The fees were £65 a term, even with the third off you got as a scholar.

His shares had been plummeting. So though I was just twelve, my life was already ruined. Instead of going to one of the finest academies in the universe, I would have to go to the local school for illiterates. The fault, my father informed us, was my mother's extravagance. 'She can't understand that it is possible to exist as a human being without having an account at Harrods.' If I went to the Illiterate Academy, I would never sit on the board of ICI, he pronounced

My school fees had been a problem before. My father had made me sit the eleven-plus, which I had scraped through. I must have been a borderline case because I wasn't accepted by Marylebone Grammar School, which was just a few hundred yards from Vincent Court. After my father had written many letters to the Divisional Officer of the London County Council – always pointing out he had an OBE and was a Doctor of Laws – I was finally offered a place at the Central Foundation of London. In the end, though, business improved and I was allowed to stay at Eaton House. To keep in with the authorities, my father sent them five guineas for the Central School Activities fund even though I wouldn't be doing any activities there.

And now I couldn't afford to attend St Paul's. He would have to go humbly back to the LCC and ask them to find me a place anywhere.

'If we do not take drastic action I may be declared bankrupt,' said my father as he tucked into his main course at the Ecu de France.

'You always exaggerate,' my mother sighed.

'Do you suppose I want to go bankrupt. Finish the *sole Véronique*. We may never again eat in a restaurant.'

'I've lost my appetite,' said my mother and pushed the fish away.

'That's because you take too many laxatives,' my father said. It was one of his favourite niggles. But he didn't let her digestion distract him for long. 'I trusted the English. During the war you could trust them. That is why I thought it would be good to come here, but they've changed. They are *crapule*.'

He went into a long harangue against a man called Berg who made raincoats. He had invested in my father's business and now wanted his money back 'at the drop of a hat'.

My mother, suddenly the good and supportive wife, pointed out that he had survived crises before – and would again. I have found letters that she wrote to him at the time and they show something was up because she often signed herself 'your obedient wife', and declared that she was 'waiting for your instructions, dear lord and master'.

But in the Ecu de France, my father refused to accept her honeyed words. 'You've never ... I am sorry to say this in front of our son ... never helped me.'

'That is not true,' she whispered so that the waiter wouldn't hear. 'And do we have to make a spectacle of ourselves in public?'

'Appearances, always appearances,' he said.

'Is it nice for our son to see us quarrelling in public?'

I see you quarrelling in private all the time, I thought but didn't say.

'When I went to your office, what did you want me to do? Clean the toilets.' Despite the I-will-do-whatever-you-say letters, my mother had never accepted the submissive-wife role that he expected her to play. With hindsight, I see that this was part of the eternal trouble between them.

'The Arabs think cleaning toilets is very honourable,' my father said.

'For Arabs maybe.' My mother had never had much time for Arabs because, like most Central Europeans, she thought they were inferior (as well as liars), though, in their defence, they could not help it. That was due to sand, sun and harems. I am sorry to say that my mother sometimes said she could understand Hitler a little!

'I've never been able to trust you ever since that business in Egypt,' my father countered.

'How many mistresses did you have in Egypt?' my mother asked.

They had stopped whispering. I was afraid that the elegant Ecu de France would laugh at us or ask us to leave. I summoned up my courage. 'I know I'm only a child but what can be done to help?' I asked.

'I know what your father will say. I spend too much, I'm too extravagant.'

'It isn't just a matter of economies,' Benjamin said with unusual calm, 'though economies always help. We need to sell something.'

Then came his *coup de grâce*, his mortal blow, though I didn't realise then how significant it would turn out to be or how much it would shape my life. He paused dramatically.

'Of course none of this would be a problem if we sold the flat on Mount Carmel,' he said.

They had owned the two-bedroom flat in Haifa for many years. My mother loved it. It was surrounded by pine trees and a small forest. From the balcony there was a view of the Mediterranean. Her brother lived half a mile away; her sister lived a short bus ride down the Carmel. She hated the idea of selling the flat, especially as she hoped we would eventually go back to Israel. I would find out soon, she said later to me, that the real reason my father wanted to sell the flat was spite. He knew she loved it. And so he did not want her to have it. But she was not going to give it up without a fight.

'It's a nice flat,' my mother said. She was trying not to cry in front of the other diners.

'It's the only thing we have to sell.'

'If only we'd bought a house here when you had the money.'

'Now I don't have money and all there is is the flat. Sooner or later it will have to be sold. You will have to go and sell it.'

'Is there nothing else?' she asked.

'Since your brother will not help me and he stole your jewels, which we also could have sold in this emergency ... No,' he said.

She dabbed her eyes. She was half crying, which exasperated my father. Everyone in the restaurant was watching, I was sure. I wanted to shrivel up and not be there.

'I'm ruined and all you can do is cry,' my father said. 'A positive element, a loyal wife, would help without making a fuss.'

'You want me to leave my son, leave my husband and go to Israel.'

'You love Israel,' my father said.

'Yes but—' She stopped.

Love didn't sway my father. He called for the bill, saying that we had better do without dessert and that he hoped there was some fruit at home. Still I noticed that my father had left a lavish tip. He noticed I noticed.

'It is not the fault of the waiter that we face financial disaster,' he said to justify himself.

Since we faced economic disaster, we could not take a cab home and we waited for a bus. All the way back, my father kept on arguing the economic and philosophical necessity of selling the flat. One of the strange things about my father was that he could be both a bully and very charming. Nobody needed a property in Israel, he pointed out. Millionaires might like to have a flat on Mount Carmel, but we were the opposite of millionaires. The other passengers on the number 15 bus ignored this revelation.

My mother did not cave in that evening. I realised over the next few weeks that she did not believe a word my father said. There were other options, but, for reasons which were sure to be immoral, he wanted to get her out of the way. I was caught in the middle of their war. My father was adamant that he would be ruined if she did not go to sell the flat. At some point, I think she sensed that it might save their marriage if she did what he wanted – or, at least, seemed to. So outwardly she became the dutiful wife and agreed to go. But not quite yet.

For weeks, Dolly discovered reasons for delaying her departure. She was not well. I could hardly be left alone to go to a new school. But she did not fool my father and he responded by starting a campaign to persuade her to go as soon as possible. I was the one and only target of his campaign. He spent more time with me than he ever had before and insisted I had to help bring her round. It was necessary to save his honour, to save the family, to save his business. Otherwise it would be the disgrace of bankruptcy. His OBE would be taken away. If I begged my mother to go in order to save our family fortunes, she couldn't refuse.

I was twelve years old. I loved my father. I believed him and I couldn't understand why my mother was being so stubborn.

'She is, I'm sorry to say, a negative element. Her parents spoiled her and she has no sense of reality.' He hinted that her obsession with gymnastics and laxatives did not help. Too much exercise of the body and the bowels was ruining her brain cells.

My father seemed very sincere and, slowly, he won me round. I started to nag her, to beg her to book a ticket. 'You're against me too,' she sighed.

I swore that I loved her – and was not against her.

The Stalin of St John's Wood

Then one afternoon, my mother told me to dress smartly as we were going to an important meeting. We were in a taxi to St John's Wood before she explained where we were headed.

Mr Berg, who had invested in my father's business, manufactured raincoats, a business which he felt was perhaps a little dull, she told me. 'Your father is always so good with words ... He promised him ... well, something.' Berg's general discontent had led him to invest money with my father's finance company. Financiers were somebodies, they had status, vision, ideas, while makers of raincoats were, at best, very rich. There was no philosophical depth in raincoats.

My mother knew that Mr Berg was, to put it mildly, a complicated man. He was one of the few millionaires to be a paid-up member of the Communist Party of Great Britain. He often made speeches on a soapbox in Lincoln's Inn Fields, speeches in which he denounced evil capitalists. Sometimes he even confessed that he was himself an evil capitalist, and smiled. 'So logically I must denounce myself, which I do,' he would add.

'He's even more *meshugge*' – 'crazier' in Yiddish – 'than your father.' My mother shook her head.

She had decided to appeal to Mrs Berg (whom she believed to be a sane person who liked poppy-seed cake) woman to woman, wife to wife. Unless Mrs Berg was a hard-hearted harpy, she would listen to our pleas and then persuade Mr Berg to be more reasonable about the repayment. If my mother could pull that off, she would not have to go to Israel to sell the flat.

We got out of the taxi at the grand block of flats overlooking Regent's Park where the Bergs lived. Mrs Berg was a plump woman with dolled-up blonde hair. She was twittery and extremely nervous as she let us in.

'Mrs Cohen, I just hope my husband does not come back ... If he does, please don't say why you have come or he'll be so angry ...'

That didn't promise well, I thought.

We sat down and my mother came straight to the point.

'Couldn't you ask your husband to wait, Mrs Berg? My husband will repay him in full with interest, but you cannot put money in a business one day and then take it out the next.' My mother sighed to emphasise the sadness of these economic transactions.

'My husband is not right in the head,' complained Mrs Berg.

'No, no, no,' my mother said tactfully.

'You don't have to live with him,' Mrs Berg said. She said she felt safe because she was sure her husband, a cricket fanatic as well as a Communist, was at Lord's for the day. She personally did not understand cricket as she had been born in Berlin. She warmed to the theme of the insanity of Mr Berg. The man preached communism, but this was by no means Berg's worst feature, she admitted. As far as she was concerned, the men could have whatever politics they wanted, and then she slipped into German. She explained that he had 'demands' in bed.

'My son understands German,' my mother pointed out, embarrassed.

'Oh my God,' Mrs Berg dropped her strudel on the carpet. 'What will he think of me? Has he been bar mitzvahed?'

Before my mother could answer, we heard footsteps. Mrs Berg tensed. She leapt to pick the strudel up from the carpet but suddenly thought better of it. A door opened. A thin man walked into the room and trod on the strudel. 'Rain stopped play,' Mr Berg announced, 'and so I came home.' He threw down his raincoat on the yellow silk settee. His mood could now be described as that of a hurricane trying hard to restrain itself.

Tornados were whipping themselves into a frenzy inside Berg and, finally, as loud on the decibel scale as my father, he screamed, 'You're entertaining the wife of a man who's trying to fiddle and diddle me.'

Mrs Berg burst into tears.

My mother was, of course, used to shouting since my father himself was a champion in the decibel department. Now in St John's Wood, the flat she loved was at stake. Dolly breathed deep and summoned all her courage.

'I came to ask your wife to appeal to her to ask you not to be too hard on my husband. He will repay you soon but—'

'I want my money and I want it now,' shouted Berg as he paced up and down his living room. As he did so, he trod bits of strudel into his carpet.

'I'll clean the carpet,' his wife said. She tried to flee to the calm of her broom cupboard.

'You sit down. I want you to hear this,' her husband said to her, and then turned to my mother. 'Your crook of a husband owes it, and he's got to pay it or I'll take him to court.'

My mother was stumped. I looked at her and then at Berg. Suddenly, I found a voice I had no idea existed.

'Is that Communist policy Mr Berg?' I asked. I realise now it was a smarty-pants scholarship boy's question.

'Don't annoy Mr Berg with rude questions, David,' my mother said.

'No, Mrs Cohen,' Berg said. He stopped pacing, stood on one leg and wiped the last bit of strudel from his shoe. Then he sat down and, for the first time, spoke rather more softly. 'It's a fair enough question. Of course, son, it is not Communist policy to ruin your fellow man because we are all comrades. But the man who lent your father money was not a Communist.'

'But you are a Communist, aren't you Mr Berg?' I said.

'Oh yes.'

'And you did lend Papa ... my father ... money which you now want at the drop of a hat.'

'Legally speaking yes, because I can't be two people. But the law is an ass. I am really two persons. People joke about how, if I make pots of money flogging raincoats, I can't be a Bolshie. That's easy to answer, son, if you know your Marx and Engels.'

'Karl Marx, grandson of two rabbis, born 1818, gave up religious Judaism, wrote *The Communist Manifesto* and caused the Russian Revolution,' I piped up.

'Good, very good. You see, Marx and Engels argued that the workers were alienated by the capitalist system. Neither of them ever had to make a bloody raincoat of course. I'm a victim of alienation like any factory worker. I was conditioned by my parents, who fled the pogroms, that I had to be rich. Work, work, work. Otherwise the Nazis would slit my throat. Do you know how boring raincoats are? Do you think making raincoats allows me to express my humanity?'

'I'd never thought about it like that,' I said.

'Of course not, because you're middle class. Have you ever worked with your hands? Or your dad? Do you know how many bloody raincoats I've stitched?'

'Don't swear in front of the child,' complained Mrs Berg.

'We're having an intellectual discussion, you stupid German cow.' He was back to shouting, but his look softened as he turned to me. 'I hate my work as much as any man down the pit. So my better self is a Communist and couldn't care less about your dad owing me money. In fact I'd lend him more out of solidarity ... But it was not Comrade Berg who lent your dad the money.'

'Who was it then?' I asked.

'Capitalist Berg whose only interest in life is, of course,

profit and shekels. He is an awful man, a product of the distortions of capitalism.'

'Don't you get confused?'

'That is what alienation does for you. I am not my true self. Except at weekends or when I skive off and go to Lord's to watch cricket. At weekends, this lucky woman lives with Comrade Berg,' he patted Mrs Berg on the knee, suggesting his insatiable sexual appetites.

Comrade Mrs Berg did her best to smile at the pat.

'I've never met anyone like you before,' I said quite sincerely.

'Most people think I'm insincere but I'm not. I lose business because lots of retailers know I'm a Communist and so they don't order my raincoats. I suspect I'm the only Jew to be blacklisted by Marks and Spencer because they know I'm a Commie.'

'Couldn't you just wait for my dad to pay?'

'I'd like to help, son, but I don't think so. Still, I like kids who ask tough questions.'

He whipped out his wallet, counted out two £5 notes and handed them to me.

'David, no!' my mother said.

'Of course he must take it. Earned it too. And it's a gift, not a loan. He's a smart boy,' Berg said.

'Thank you,' I said.

'I will send you some leaflets about the Party. We could do with kids like you in the Young Communists.'

'Thank you for being so nice to my son,' my mother said. She could see there was no arguing with Red Berg. He walked us to the door and said, 'You should be proud of your son, Mrs Cohen.'

She smiled nervously, took my arm and hurried down the stairs.

'He's crazier than your father. He wants to turn you into Stalin,' my mother said when we were safely in the street. She hailed a cab. Once we were inside, she told me that if I loved her, I must never tell my father where we had been. 'Promise, David,' she said.

'Didn't he know we were coming?'

'He will be *fou furieux*, if he finds out,' she said. Mad with anger. 'You must promise not to tell him.'

I was scared that he would ask me on my honour whether or not we had met Berg. But my mother was pleading, and so I promised.

The next few days passed without any dramas. But I did notice that every evening when we had finished dinner, and my father said nothing, my mother seemed very relieved. After ten days, she thought she was safe. Then one evening ...

'You had to humiliate me,' my father shouted the moment he got in the door. When I went to help him take his coat off (my father never came home quietly. He would demand help getting his coat off, help putting his hat away), he turned away from me in fury. He had found out by accident and it was my fault. My father and Berg had met to discuss when Berg would get his money back. The meeting had been hostile. 'I will sue you for everything,' Berg had said, 'and I'm sorry if that upsets your son. He's a very clever lad.'

My father loomed over me and hit me. His violence felt even less deserved than when he had read out Mr Buckland's letter. I hadn't decided to visit Berg. My father continued to shout while he was hitting me.

'At first I assumed Berg had heard about the scholarship,' my father shouted.

'Stop please, Papa,' I said.

He couldn't stop himself trying to hit me again.

'Please stop,' I begged.

Then my father laughed bitterly. 'But he said he would never congratulate anyone who went to a public school. And then I discovered why you went to see my enemy.'

'I was trying to help,' my mother said.

'The only thing you were trying to do was not to sell the flat,' my father continued shouting. Then he turned to me. 'And you took his money. I hope you kept it. We may need it to buy food.' He was calmer now. Hitting me had restored him to some sort of balance.

'Berg listened to me, Papa.'

'Like I would listen to his son. You were precocious, an object of curiosity. It didn't help.'

'I knew you'd blame me,' my mother snuffled.

'There's no point in crying. Tears make no differences to philistines like Berg. He doesn't understand the first thing about Communism by the way. I have had enough of your delaying, *madame*. You have to go and sell the flat. The only thing that will pacify him is money I don't have. I hope you've cooked something edible.'

The authority in my father's voice was final.

The rest of the evening he refused to speak. She kept on saying she had tried to help and that my father was being unjust. He retreated into silence, something rare for him.

By going to see Mrs Berg behind my father's back, my mother had put herself deeply in the wrong. I didn't help her because I felt ashamed that I had conspired against my father. As a result, she was going to have to go Israel. She even began to discuss booking a flight. When my father insisted it was a matter of survival, she didn't argue.

My father also softened a little. 'I know you don't want to sell it, Dolly. I know it has sentimental value for you, but *c'est la guerre*.'

It was war – us against the rest of the world.

Now that he had her on the run, my father never lost an opportunity to nag me or to nag her. He wanted her to go 'with a good heart'. He fed me arguments constantly. I had to tell her that going to Israel would do her good, that I was a big boy and that I would not miss her for a few weeks. Her father, my grandfather, who was a practical man who understood the realities of commerce, would have understood the need to sell the flat *in extremis*. 'And we are in *extremis*. In more extreme *extremis* than I have ever known,' he said.

But my father was also more understanding than he had ever been before. When we were alone, he said to me that I had to be mature. I had to understand that 'It is not her fault. Her mother and father protected her from the facts of life so she never believes that money problems are real. She thinks I have secret bank accounts – because her father had plenty of those – and that if I don't have money to throw around, it's because I'm Harpagon. You know who Harpagon is?'

'The miser in *L'Avare*, the play by Molière.'

'Good. If I had a shilling to spare I'd give it you, popski.'

'Has it got worse, Papa?' I asked nervously – as if the financial situation were a patient whose condition might have deteriorated.

The financial situation was on its last legs, my father said. 'I have told Berg that your mother is going to Israel to sell our property and that has made him pause for a bit, but he's the kind of man who will not pause for long.'

My father needed an ally and so he paid me far more attention than usual. He took me to tea at Fortnum and Mason – which we seemed to be able to afford despite imminent bankruptcy. He knew I loved the chocolate milkshakes at their soda fountain. When he was in this mood, he forgot about the laxatives that were killing off my mother's brain cells. 'Even though she is an intelligent woman and there's nothing wrong with her brain, she refuses to see that one plus one make two.' I was flattered to be treated as an adult in waiting and, gradually, he convinced me. Maybe my mother, whom I adored, *was* being unreasonable.

I started to ask her questions about why it was so hard for her to go to Israel.

'I see your father has won you over,' she said sadly, early one evening while I was doing my homework. 'I didn't expect my son who says he loves me to—'

But she didn't finish her sentence.

'I only said—' I started, and didn't finish my sentence.

'You said enough, David. Your father could always talk and charm anyone when it suits him. I'm not surprised his son should believe every word he says.'

As if I were a total twelve-year-old innocent.

'It would suit him to have me far away,' she said.

'Why?'

She just shrugged.

'Perhaps he has done bad things and lied, but that doesn't mean he is lying now,' I said. 'He does owe Berg money and Berg is strange. Going to Israel is not like going to the moon. You'll only be a phone call away. I can ring you, Mama. Maybe it is the best thing to do. Please.'

'The *only* thing to do, according to your father – and now you. Or we'll have to beg in the streets,' she laughed bitterly. And then she started to cry.

The son she adored had become one of the men who betrayed her.

'I wish you wouldn't cry,' I said.

At night I could hear them talk in bed. My father shouted less than usual, which made me glad, though I couldn't help wondering whether it was all part of his campaign. I must add one thing about my father. He could get furious with my mother, and, a few times, he threatened to hit her, but he never did. For all her complaints about him, she never said to me that he had been physically violent towards her. He had some strange but fundamental ethical code that made it acceptable to lie, cheat and shout – but it would be unforgivable to hit a woman. So I bore the brunt of his outbursts.

His charm and bully offensive finally worked.

Late in August, my mother gave in. She would go in the first week of September.

We patched up a kind of peace for the few days before she left. My father booked her on a flight to Tel Aviv on a Sunday morning. That way he could take her to the airport without losing time that should have been spent working. At the airport he even bought her a bottle of perfume, but when they reached Departures, he embraced her reluctantly. He let her lean forward to kiss him on the cheek. Did he deflect her kiss from the lips to his cheek? I couldn't be sure, but I thought he did.

We carried her hand luggage to the final boarding gate.

I hugged my mother fervently and promised a long list of promises:

To behave.

To look after my father.

To make sure my father looked after me.

To eat properly.

To write at least every second day so she would know everything. (She said that to me often when we were alone and hinted that my father would be up to something the instant she was on the plane.)

To take my clothes to the dry-cleaners.

To make sure the fridge was kept clean.

Not to forget her.

To make a good impression at school.

To go to synagogue every Friday.

To light the candles in the flat on the Sabbath.

'You'll miss the plane,' my father said impatiently.

'Oh,' she sighed, and she hugged me fiercely – all her love squeezed into one embrace. Then, more shyly, she embraced my father again and walked through to Passport Control.

I waited till I couldn't see her.

'Come on, popski,' my father said.

'Can't we wait till the plane takes off?'

'No, I have work to do.'

On the coach back to London, he wanted to read the paper but I plagued him.

'How long will she be gone?' I asked.

'A few weeks. It's a flat in a very good location. And a good time to sell. Lots of people will want to buy it.'

With that, he returned to the vital business of looking at the *Financial Times*.

When we got back to Vincent Court he buried himself in important-looking files. At the end of the afternoon he took out his stamp collection and shook his head sadly. The Stanley Gibbons catalogue said it was worth £10,000 but when he had offered it to them for sale, they said they would only pay £1,500. 'I am going to sell the most valuable stamps,' he said, 'so we at least have petty cash.'

In 1960, the average wage in Britain was under £600 a year.

Benjamin slammed the stamp albums shut and looked at me across the dining-room table. Words of wisdom and command were about to be uttered, I knew. 'You must not become a mama's boy. Psychologically and morally, being away from your mother will toughen you up,' he said.

I didn't realise how true that would be.

Waiting to Go to St Paul's

I had spent nights away from my mother before. When I was six, I had been sent to a holiday camp in the Swiss Alps. I hated it and ran away, and so the camp had to ring my parents to come and get me. I couldn't get to sleep the night she left. I worked out where the plane would be, when she would land, when she would reach Haifa. In the morning my father was cheerful and said I should accompany him to his office in Jermyn Street. Miraculously, my father had found the money to pay the fees for one term at least, so I was going to St Paul's in five days' time. In order not to disgrace myself I had to be on top of the international situation. I could use the time to read the papers.

Life in the office was very quiet. My father often had to go to meetings and Evi often went with him. I was left alone in the office. There was nothing to do. The phone never rang. No wonder secretaries canoodled with their bosses. They had so much time to kill.

Once when Evi was not there, my father said, 'She's a good girl. Not that intelligent, but willing. Women ought to be willing.'

Had that been the trouble with my mother? She was not willing enough?

Evi came back into the room and sat down at her desk. My father seemed not to notice and continued at me, 'Your mother never lifted a finger to help me.'

'She went to Israel because you asked.'

I didn't like talking about her in front of Evi.

'Only because I yelled and threatened. Do you think I like to live like that? I apologise. I don't mean to insult your mother in front of you and Evi, even if it happens to be the truth.'

Was this the kind of development my mother wanted me to write to her about? I could picture her reaction. She'd sigh that Benjamin was being unjust to her again but what could she expect? He was an Arab at heart and dreamt of having four wives.

It felt good to hear my mother's voice in my head. I had steeled myself not to miss her too much. I knew letters took at least four days to get to England from Israel so I was not disappointed not to receive one immediately. But it was not so easy to stay so brave for long.

Two days before I started at St Paul's, I persuaded my father to let me stay at home because I had to make sure I had everything I needed for my new school. The day went very slowly. I listened to the radio, went to Selfridges, walked around Hyde Park.

At five o'clock my father rang. Business meetings were keeping him at the office. I should get something to eat because he didn't want me to complain of malnutrition. An hour later, he rang again to say that a potential client had arrived from Malta and he would not be back till very late.

'You're old enough to be alone for a few hours, you're not a baby.' Being a baby was, of course, the supreme sin. 'Your mother has turned you into a baby because her parents *pesevke* turned her into a baby.' He hoped that I was paying attention to the political situation in the Middle East and in the Himalayas, where the Indians and Chinese were rattling their sabres at each other.

I assured him I was on top of the news from the subcontinent.

By eleven o'clock there was still no sign of my father. I strained to hear footsteps. Every time I heard a car stop I went to the window and looked to see whether it was a cab and he was getting out of it. He used cabs now. The 'liquidity crisis', as he put it, had eased because he had sold some of the stamps. But no cab dropped him off.

There were two rooms in the flat from which you could not hear what was happening outside on the street – my small bedroom and the bathroom. I brushed my teeth walking around the flat so that I wouldn't miss the sound of a cab stopping or of my father's footsteps coming home. I brushed them slowly up and down as our dentist had told me to. I prayed my father would come back soon. I told myself that if I recited in chronological order the kings and queens of England, he would be back by the time I got to George V.

I got to George V, did the dates for Edward VII, did the dates for George VI …

There was still no sign of him. The magic hadn't worked. There was complete silence, eerie silence. I got into my pyjamas and tied the cord in an elaborate bow.

Half past eleven was not so late for adults who were dealing with new clients from Malta, I told myself.

I got into bed. The sheets were freezing. I'd never before gone to sleep in an empty house with no one else there. When we lived in Israel I used to hold my cousin's hand as I was falling asleep.

I told myself, yet again, that I must not worry if my father was not back.

I felt thirsty and got up to get a glass of water. The kitchen was near the front door and I listened for footsteps again. But there was silence, only silence. I went to have a pee. I walked back to the kitchen. It was now 11.45. I couldn't sleep so I took out the volume of the *Encyclopaedia Britannica* and read about Charles I, reigned 1625–49, who caused the Civil War because he was stubborn, insisted on the Divine Right of kings and wouldn't listen to MPs (who had no expenses to fiddle in those days).

I could hear my mother's voice: Your father always says he's working late when whatever it is he's doing, it's not work. I wouldn't trust your father as far as I could throw a cedar of Lebanon. What kind of business keeps you late, Benjamin? Money business or monkey business?

I wondered where my father might be. At dinner in a hotel, drinking in a bar or with a woman my mother would call '*une des ces femmes*'? From somewhere there came to mind a phone number. I knew whose it was. It was Evi's.

I hesitated, picked up the phone, put it down.

If you rang and said you were worried about your father because he was not at home, no one could blame you. Your father should be home, should be ashamed of himself – leaving you alone. Till midnight. Past midnight.

A normal son is worried about his father. Accidents occur. Fatalities clog up the Central Line all the time.

So I picked up the phone again and dialled.

'Who is that?'

I recognised Evi's voice at the other end of the line. I did not reply.

'Who is that?' she repeated.

I wondered if I should put the phone down.

There was a shuffle. The phone was being handed over. My father had a very distinctive voice but it was muffled now.

'I warn you that elements who make obscene phone calls go to jail. It is a serious offence and carries three years in prison at least.'

Not many people refer to 'elements', but it was one of my father's favourite words. Though his voice was muffled, I knew it was him. He was miles away because Evi lived on the borders of Kent.

Would I be sent to jail, I wanted to ask, just because I wanted to know where my father was. I nearly said, 'I'm glad I found you.' But I thought better of it and said nothing.

The line went dead at the other end. I put the phone down quietly. It was possible, of course, that the business meeting with the Maltese had adjourned to Evi's flat. But I was my mother's son – and she had told me enough of the ways of the world for me to know how unlikely that was.

Almost as soon as I put the phone down, it rang. It might be smart not to answer it at once. I walked towards the bedroom and then back to the small table in the living room where the phone stood. I counted till there were eight rings. It mustn't seem that I was waiting by it. On the tenth ring I answered, and I added a big yawn.

'Is that you, David?' my father asked angrily. His voice was not muffled now.

Who bloody else would be here? I thought but didn't say.

'Papa where are you? I was asleep.'

'Are you sure you were asleep?'

'Yes … Is something wrong? Where are you?'

My father did not answer the question but asked, 'What have you been doing?'

'Sleeping.'

'My meeting has gone on very late but it's over now. Though I can't really afford a taxi I'll take one back to the flat.'

I wanted to trap my father, to get him to admit where he really was. My mother would be proud of me. But I couldn't think of a way of doing it that would not betray the fact I had rung Evi's. 'I'll go back to sleep,' I said, the good and obedient son who did not ask tricky questions.

An hour later, I heard the cab draw up, the door slam, the front door open, the footsteps I'd been waiting for.

When my father walked in, I was lying in bed, pretending to sleep. He sat at the end of the bed and said I had to understand. He had to work hard and business meetings were sometimes very complicated. The Maltese were a difficult lot. They liked to drink whisky, which they thought was an essential part of doing business in England. He kissed me gently on the top of my head, said goodnight and went into his bedroom.

I still couldn't fall asleep. Later in the night, very quietly, I got up. I sat in the living room and looked at the street. The sound of my father snoring from his bedroom was comforting. Then something magical happened. A number of horses trotted past outside the window. The mounted police were riding down Seymour Place on their way to Hyde Park for a dawn gallop. The clip-clop of their hooves was hypnotic, calming. I went back to bed more at peace than I'd expected to be.

I was still waiting to hear from my mother. I also knew I had to write to her to explain what had happened. Since I was going to tell her part of the truth at least, I had to make certain my father did not get to see the letter. I wrote a complicated letter in my head.

When my father woke up, I told him I wanted to stay at home to make sure I was perfectly prepared for my first day at school. As soon as he left for work, I wrote to my mother. I explained he had come home very late, but I did not say I thought he had been at Evi's. I sent the letter express. It was still only eleven o'clock. I had the rest of the day to get through and I didn't want to think too much about what had happened. I decided to go to Lord's. I half hoped that I might run into Mr Berg, but I didn't. It was a Wednesday, and on Wednesdays he was a capitalist, making and selling his raincoats.

First Day of School

I left Lord's at five o'clock because I didn't want my father to find out I had been to a cricket match. It was a good move because he was back home just after six. He had decided to be home early as this was the night before I started at my new school. He was in a good mood and full of advice. He told me – and I always loved it when he confided something of his past – about his first day at school.

'On the first day the monks offered me chocolate if I converted but I resisted.'

'I don't think they do that at St Paul's.'

'Never be ashamed of what you are,' my father said.

We both knew that I had had to do very well to get into the school because there was a Jewish quota, which meant that St Paul's never took more than 10 per cent of Jewish pupils.

My father said that, as a treat that night, we would go to Harry Gold's kosher restaurant just off Baker Street. We mustn't spend too much but I could have viennas and latkes, the potato pancakes I loved. He had high hopes of the Maltese.

In the morning, my father made sure I looked respectable and that my tie was straight. I have always had trouble with ties. He helped me fix the silver fish on my lapel. To wear the fish was one of the privileges that the 153 scholars of St Paul's enjoyed. 'The fish is, of course, a Christian symbol because

Christ called his disciples fishers of men.' It did not occur to either of us that I should not wear it because I was a Jew.

My father walked me down to the bus stop at Marble Arch and waited till the number 73 came. He gave me a hug just before I got on. It was my first day at the big school and I was nervous.

My anxiety zoomed up as it seemed less and less likely that I'd get to school on time. The traffic was jammed all the way to Hyde Park Corner. Knightsbridge was clogged, and all the traffic lights were red. It was already 8.24 by the Harvey Nichols clock by Knightsbridge Tube.

The bus driver didn't have the slightest idea of the hell I was living through on the top deck. I had to be in school by 8.30 and I couldn't see how we could possibly get to Hammersmith in six minutes.

After Knightsbridge, the traffic did flow quickly, but when we got to Kensington High Street, we reverted to snail's pace. At Eaton House it didn't matter if I was late because I was the head boy. Here I'd be in for the chop.

Finally, we passed Olympia. I rushed down and jumped off at the request stop in front of St Paul's before the bus had quite stopped. I ran past the pretty little gatehouse up the stairs into the school's gothic entrance hall.

'New boy,' barked a giant prefect who stood waiting to discipline latecomers.

'Yes.'

'Name?'

'David Cohen.'

'You're late … Well, get going.'

I had no idea where to go. He gestured angrily in the direction of the school hall and I ran.

'Don't run,' he yelled after me. 'It's against the rules.'

At the entrance to the main hall, there was another

prefect – and he was in no better mood. 'Do you realise how late you are?'

'Sorry, traffic was bad,' I said.

'Never blame the traffic. It's so banal. Tomorrow you'll report at 8.15 to the prefects' room and do a hundred lines before assembly. You'll translate "the bus crawled towards the Vestal virgins" into Latin.'

I had been terrified I was going to be caned – something I had managed to avoid in five years at Eaton House. I almost shouted for joy.

But my joy didn't last long. Those who had designed the main hall and chapel of St Paul's knew about the architecture of power. The masters sat on a raised platform. A special pulpit, raised even higher, allowed the High Master or special guests like the Archbishop of Canterbury or Montgomery of Alamein (our most famous old boy) to glare down at the boys. The High Master, the Reverend Gilkes, was very tall and prided himself on his eagle eye.

He spotted me, stopped speaking and thundered. 'What is your name boy?'

Six hundred heads swivelled to look at me.

'You, a scholar because I can see your fish, you are shuffling in late trying to look insignificant, what is your name?'

'Cohen, sir,' I spluttered.

'Are you proud of being late on your first day at school?'

'N-no sir.'

'Don't splutter, boy,' Gilkes thundered again.

'No,' I stammered, 'no … sir.'

'Was it bad traffic, trouble tying your tie, which looks a shade crooked, or trouble waking up because you ate too much last night?'

'Traffic was terrible, sir.'

'It always was in ancient Rome, too. Dung on the streets.

But that did not stop the conscientious schoolboy – what is "schoolboy" in Latin?'

'*Pupillari*, sir.' Thank God I could remember.

'In Rome you would have been flogged. But we are more forgiving. You have wasted two minutes of the time of about six hundred other human beings in distracting us from our thinking on this the first day of term. We are all two minutes closer to death. Are you proud of that?'

'I'm so sorry, sir.'

'Organise yourself and your parents more efficiently in future.'

'Yes, sir,' I said trying not to splutter or stammer.

The High Master picked up where he had left off. The privilege of coming to one of the greatest schools in the country meant we had responsibilities. The school demanded the highest effort of work, discipline and punctuality. He was pleased to note that only one pupil was late, though that pupil was one too many.

When the time for prayers came, Jews were excused from assembly. There were maybe sixty of us because of the school's Jewish quota. One of the prefects took us to a large room where we were supposed to read. Ten minutes later, a bell sent us scurrying to class.

'One of our class was negligent enough to be late,' said the Latin master at the start of my first class. He reminded us that we were the crème de la crème and that he expected the highest standards of work, punctuality and accuracy in Latin 'unseens'. We would begin with Caesar and *De Bello Gallico*. Caesar did not conquer the known world by turning up late for his battles, he added.

Caesar hadn't had to cope with the traffic at Hyde Park Corner, I thought but didn't say.

Starting at a new school is never easy, but I had not been

told that one of the rules of St Paul's was that you had to join the Cadet Corps. I would have to wear a uniform every Monday, learn to drill and learn to shoot. The Battle of Waterloo might have been won on the playing fields of Eton, but the Battle of El Alamein – and indeed the Second World War – had been won at St Paul's thanks to Field Marshal Montgomery. On the afternoon of that first day, we were given an introductory lecture about the Cadet Corps and told that the great Montgomery would be inspecting us later in the term.

I didn't relish the idea of playing soldiers, not because I was a pacifist but because I suspected the uniform would itch, and I had a sinking feeling that I was not cut out for military manoeuvres.

Otherwise, though, it was not a bad day. The work was not too hard and I was looking forward to telling my father that I had coped. I let myself into the block, checked the letter box and, finally, there was a letter from my mother. It was very short, which disappointed me. She did not have a buyer for the flat yet, but the weather was fine. She missed me and hoped I was well. 'I have no news from your father, of course, but I would be very interested in knowing how he is and what he is doing,' she added. She had underlined the last four words. She had written no more than a page. Since she had left I had written six long letters – and every one begged her to come back soon.

My father got home around seven. He was livid when I told him I had been late to school. That was the fault of my mother's bad genes and he would make bloody sure I was there on time the next day. He was yelling and his face was flushed red. This was the way he looked when he hit me. Without thinking, I backed away from him.

To my surprise, he didn't grab hold of me and start

slapping me. He paused and took a deep breath. Being late wasn't the end of the world, he said. I had started as a pupil in one of Britain's great schools and, even though finances were frail, we would eat out that evening. We had no choice, in fact. There was only bread and cheese in the flat.

I decided to take no risks the next morning. I was at the bus stop at 7.15, so early that the traffic was light. I was waiting outside the prefects' room by 7.45. I had looked in the dictionary and the best Latin translation I could find for 'bus' was *vehiculum*. The prefects laughed at me a little but I didn't mind. I had expected much worse.

I settled quickly into the routine at school. The masters were less eccentric than they had been at prep school. No one flung chalk or lighted matches. There was one master who had an artificial leg. At Eaton House he might well have unscrewed it and thrown it at us, but St Paul's did not encourage such idiosyncrasies. Boys were caned, but only by the High Master, who was not known to have a taste for meting out such punishment. He really meant it when he said that it would hurt him too.

Usually you start to make friends during your first weeks at a new school, but I was nervous. I had no idea what to say if people asked me about my parents so I stayed aloof. No one seemed to mind or tried particularly hard to make friends with me.

And then came the first Monday of the Cadet Corps. We collected our uniforms and, before we put them on, one of the masters who had the rank of captain addressed us.

'Some of you,' he warned, 'will have mothers who offer to press your shirts and crease your trousers. Some of the dafter maters may even offer to shine your boots. No decent soldier lets a woman touch his kit. Your kit is your own sacred responsibility.'

We were sent off to change into the uniforms. The trouble was that I had never put one on before. The shirt and trousers were normal and I got into those fine. But no one explained what you had to do with the belt, garters and gaiters. My boots were too tight. Three times I tried to get the gaiters on but they slipped through my fingers. Some of the other boys were watching me and I wondered when they would start laughing.

'You are a total wreck. Your belt is on back to front, you might as well be wearing your gaiters on your head and your boots are muddy,' said a corporal who was all of sixteen years old.

'I'm sorry,' I replied.

'Sorry? You're in the army now, you little turd,' he snapped. I did not know what 'turd' meant. 'I am going to be bloody nice to you since it's your first day in the Corps. I want to see you at oh-eight-hundred hours next Monday properly dressed in uniform – with your boots so shiny I can eat off them.'

'Yes sir,' and I turned to go.

'You salute me before you move.'

I shambled a salute.

'I know one thing about you, Cohen,' he laughed. 'You are not Israel's secret weapon.'

I wanted to run away and cry but I couldn't. I was desperate to tell my father and to ask for his help. He had been in the navy after all, though he was never that clear about his rank. I was worried that he would be livid – but he might not be. In my head, going back home on the 73, I set out the reasons for telling him and the reasons for not telling him. I had not decided which it would be by the time I walked up Seymour Place towards the flat.

The Blue Suitcase Saga

The flats at Vincent Court had a porter, a thin Scot called Watson who, my father had explained, had a taste for whisky.

Watson was mopping the entrance hall when I got home.

'I didn't expect to see you. I thought you were going on a trip.'

'I don't think my school would like that. We've just started the term.'

'You never know with foreigners,' he smirked.

I walked past him and looked in the letter box. There was no letter from my mother.

I opened the door of the flat and sat down in the living room. For some reason, I got up and walked into my parents' bedroom. I was surprised to see their big blue suitcase on the bed.

That was odd. I was still upset from my run-in at the Corps. I wondered why on earth the suitcase was out. I picked it up. It was heavy and obviously full.

My mother would want me to look inside. 'Papa,' I shouted. I knew he wasn't in the flat but I wanted to make sure the coast was clear. There was a security chain on the front door, and I put it on. My father couldn't surprise me now.

I went back into the bedroom, looked at the suitcase and pushed the locks so that they flew up. What I saw did not make sense. The suitcase contained three of my father's suits, a number of his shirts, underpants and ties. I stared at them.

Then there was a furious shout at the front door. It my father. He had tried to open the front door and found that the chain was on.

I slammed the lid shut but I was shaking. I didn't snap both locks shut. I knew I had to be quick.

'Who the hell is in there?' he shouted.

I just hoped he wouldn't notice one of the locks was not secure. I breathed deep and yelled, 'Just coming Papa.'

'I was on the toilet,' I said, as I took the chain off and let him in.

'Why was the chain on?'

'Sometimes I get a bit worried when I'm here on my own.'

He walked past me and into his bedroom. I tried to appear casual.

'I've got a lot of homework to do,' I said.

'Let me give you some advice about spying. I've told you I did intelligence work during the war.'

'Yes, Papa.'

'When we looked in people's suitcases, we were very careful to shut them properly after we had looked inside,' he said quite calmly. 'I shut both locks and now one lock is open. Look.'

I bent down to look and he hit me. I shrieked in pain and surprise.

'I just wondered about the suitcase.'

'You were spying on me.' He wasn't the least bit calm now. He was shouting and had gone red in the face.

'No, Papa, please.'

This time he didn't stop for breath and reconsider.

'Don't lie as well. You were spying on me.' He slapped me hard again. I started to cry.

'I came home, and the porter said something about travelling … I just wanted to know what was going on.'

'You were spying on me. Just like your mother told you to.'

'She didn't tell me to spy on you,' I lied.

'If you lie to me again, I will hit you so hard you will be really sorry.'

'Where are you going? Why?'

'You sound more and more like your mother. Hysterical. Is it a nice thing for a son to do? Spy on his father? Men should stick together. Sons should be loyal to their fathers. If my father told me a secret, I'd die rather than betray him.'

Paranoia, the fixed pattern of his suspicion. I had to be with him or I was against him.

'Is there a secret then?'

'If there was, could I trust you?'

'Oh yes.'

'I don't believe you.' He paused to consider the delicate issue of whether his son was really with him or might turn against him. He yo-yoed because sometimes he would concede that, of course, a son had to defend his mother, even if that meant defending her against his father. Not that he, Benjamin, the father was unreasonable or had done anything wrong. He was more sinned against than sinning, sinned against by the monstrous ranks of the devious, dishonest Cappon family, my mother's family. At all other times, a son's duty was 100 per cent clear – total loyalty to his father.

He spread out his arms wide and said softly, 'I have to go to Manchester for a few days on business.'

'Does that mean I have to go with you?'

'You can't miss school, popski.' He was all reason and charm suddenly.

'But what will I do?' I was terrified at the prospect of being alone.

'I am sure Evi would let you stay with her.'

He knew I could not get to St Paul's from where she lived on the borders of Kent. He also knew that I would not want to go there under any circumstances.

'Will you be gone long?' I asked, defeated.

'Two days, three days. And of course I'll phone you.'

'But who is going to stay with me?' I asked.

'I'm going to give the porter a nice tip so he will keep an eye on you. He is a bit of an alcoholic but I'll read him the riot act.'

'I've never been alone for a night before.'

'I know, popski,' he smiled. 'But I was sent alone to Jerusalem when I was your age and I managed.' He paused. 'You are almost a man and I'm proud of you.' He took out two £5 notes. 'I don't want you to run short of money,' he said.

'Thank you.'

'But I don't want your mother to panic and she *will* panic if she thinks I have had to leave you on your own.'

So there was a secret, a secret to keep from her.

'She'd worry, which is natural. But you are not a baby. So do I have your word of honour?'

I knew what the word of honour was – not to write to my mother to say he had gone off for a few days on his own.

'Yes.'

'On your honour?'

'On my honour,' I promised.

He was calmer now I'd given in. He looked me straight in the eye. Those who could not look a man in the eye were deceitful and devious. 'I don't want to leave you alone, popski, but these are difficult times, my son, for making a crust. Perhaps I should have told you this might happen, but an economic opportunity has come up. Very suddenly.' He was smiling now. 'It would be criminally negligent not to try to make the most of an economic opportunity.'

'I suppose if I need something the porter will help.' I thought it best to sound chirpy.

'I am very proud of you, popski,' he smiled.

Proud meant presents. He took out another £5 note for 'genuine emergencies'.

'Or chocolates,' he laughed. 'You really are not a child any more.'

This was a compliment. Now that I was Not a Child, I could be allowed into the mysteries of adult life, though I suspected this would be one more partial version of the truth.

Funnily enough some of these new economic opportunities were linked to Berg. 'You really did make a big impression on him, popski.' Berg's contacts lacked education, my father added, but they did want to broaden their horizons and organise their investments in fields other than raincoats. 'So they have asked me to set up a company,' he explained.

'In Manchester?'

He nodded. It always rained in Manchester, so it was a Mecca for the raincoat brigade, it seemed.

'When are you leaving?'

'Now. I came back to see you. I must catch the train soon.'

So he had decided to do it anyway. It didn't matter what I felt. I didn't want to let him go and said I'd go with him to the station.

'You stay and do your homework. I don't like emotional scenes when I leave. I'll be back in two or three days.'

I watched my father drag the suitcase down and waited outside while he hailed the cab. I heard him say Euston Station, the station you needed for Manchester.

I watched the cab drive off. To get from Vincent Court to

Euston you had to drive north up Seymour Place to the Marylebone Road and then turn right. I was a little surprised when the cab did a U-turn and headed south towards Marble Arch. I waved at the cab heading off in its unexpected direction and then trudged back inside the flat. I made myself a promise. I would make the best of it, and when he came back, my father would be proud of me. It would like one of those Second World War adventures.

It was a doddle, Major. All the other children might have love and homes and someone to tuck them in at night, but we kids of the secret orphan brigade do not need mollycoddling. We muddle through and please don't call us heroes. We're just ordinary twelve-year-olds doing our best for Queen, Dad and Country.

At least I would not now have the worry of waiting for my father to come home late at night. I went into the small kitchen, cut myself a chunk of bread and some cheese and put the kettle on. I'd have some beef stock, which was very comforting, while I did my homework. Then I decided not to do my homework at once. I switched on the television, promising myself that I would only watch for an hour. After that I would read about the spice trade to the East Indies and the devious tricks that British captains used to fiddle the poor Malays out of their pepper. I also had an essay to write on Benedict and Beatrice as we were doing *Much Ado About Nothing* for O level (at St Paul's you did O levels a year early). But there was no one to tell me when I had to do it as long as I got it in on time.

In the past I was always so grateful when the flat was quiet. It meant Benjamin and Dolly were not fighting. I switched off the television and now there was utter silence. I wasn't sure whether I liked it or not. I did my homework, brushed my teeth, had a minor discussion with God on the subject of whether it was fair that I had been left here alone and tried to go to sleep. But I couldn't. I now knew how I felt about the silence: I hated it.

I went into my parents' bedroom and lugged the big radio they had into my room. I turned it on softly and I listened to the *Shipping Forecast*. I must have finally dozed off to reports of how bad the winds were at Finisterre.

Because I hadn't switched it off, the radio woke me up early the next morning. First there was 'Rule Britannia, Britannia rule the waves', followed by a jolly tune to which (I now realise) can be sung the words of 'What Shall We Do with the Drunken Sailor?' Somebody at the BBC must have thought it funny to play this alongside the *Shipping Forecast*.

I was at the 73 bus stop by 7.15. I got to school fifteen minutes later and had to wait for the prefects to open the doors. I wondered how they would react if I told them I had slept all alone in a flat in the West End and that I did not expect any adult to be home tonight or the next night, or perhaps even the night after that. The Latin master, Mr Train, had said that boys should bring him their problems, but I suspected that he meant problems understanding Caesar, Tacitus or Livy rather than anything truly personal.

'You don't seem entirely with us,' Mr Train griped at me. He had good antennae but they were all trained on the ancient world. 'Explain the main policies used by Agricola in his governorship of Britain and what his aims were,' he said.

I remembered enough Agricola to get by. I got through maths and history without telling a soul that I was now an orphan – even if it were only for two or three days. I was sure I was the only child in the school who would be home alone that night. In the flat I could cry, but at school I didn't just feel sorry for myself. I was also excited by my secret. And I realised it was a big secret. I had to be careful the school did not find out. Of course, it never occurred to St Paul's that one of its pupils had been abandoned in the West End by his parents.

My father rang that night to make sure I was all right. I realised somehow that there was no point begging him to come home quicker so I might as well make him feel proud. I told him that school had been fine, which was true – I had given a good account of how Agricola had ruled Britain – and this was untrue – that the Cadet Corps was a calamity as usual. I said I had cooked myself scrambled eggs – which was not true, as I had started to worry when the butter I was sizzling started to make weird noises. I took the pan off the cooker and had bread, cheese, fruit and chocolate. I said – true – that I had done my work. That was always bloody true: homework as therapy, bury your troubles in the Tudors and Stuarts and Latin unseens.

'How is Manchester?' I asked.

'Manchester is very busy. I will see you Friday.'

I had hoped he would be back before then.

'Papa,' I hesitated, 'will you ring me again tomorrow?'

'If I can, David, if I can. You are quite old enough to look after yourself for seventy-two hours.'

'Yes, Papa,' I said.

'Good. Well go to sleep early and remember the early bird catches the banana. And if there is any emergency, get the porter. I've given him a big enough tip.'

Before I could prolong any goodbyes, he put the phone down. The flat seemed so empty – more like a tomb than a luxury apartment in the West End.

That Friday my father, evidently back in London, told me to come to his office. We would start the weekend with a good dinner and he had bought tickets for a play. *Uncle Vanya* was always worth seeing. It was obvious that things were looking up because there was a new secretary, Mrs Brown. She was in her late thirties and much more elegant than Evi.

'The situation in Manchester is promising,' my father told me.

I felt so happy, so relieved to be with him.

'You have been a very good boy.' He patted me on the head. 'The next few weeks are vital for our survival so you can sit by Mrs Brown and do your homework. No business can survive if its employees start the weekend at four o'clock. And that is even true for the boss,' he smiled.

My father went back into his office.

'You know your father is a wonderful man,' Mrs Brown said.

'Oh yes.'

'You're lucky to have a father like that,' and she smiled too.

I wondered if she had joined the harem of sex-retaries, though presumably if caught in flagrante, she would not try to wrap herself in the *Times of India*. But then I remembered … Decent boys who do not betray their fathers do not think like that. I asked Mrs Brown if there were any chocolate biscuits on the premises.

She found me some.

Later we went to the theatre. *Uncle Vanya* was moving. My father said we would have to make do with a snack as he needed a good night's sleep. Things were not going as well as he made out in the office, he confessed, but he needed to keep up appearances, especially for Mrs Brown. 'I have high hopes she will turn out to be a positive element,' he said. Nothing had come of the Maltese, who were, it turned out, degenerates. He was also angry because he had heard from my mother, and 'I don't have to be Sherlock Holmes to realise she is not lifting a finger to sell the flat.' Given her family history, he was sure there was all kinds of monkey business going on. 'Monkey business' was a phrase they both liked.

'Mama is trying, I'm sure,' I said.

'Popski, a son should defend his mother,' and he smiled, 'but you don't know all the facts.'

With that, he went to bed.

Next week he would have to spend more time in Manchester, he told me the next morning. But that would not be a problem, would it? I had coped, hadn't I?

Memory tries to cheat us and, at times, I have doubted that the events I'm describing took place. But my father was a lawyer by training and lawyers like to write things down. He and my mother liked to quote a Latin tag, *'verba volens, scripta manens'* – what is spoken flies away, what is written remains. In making sense of my past and writing this book I have been helped by the notes, letters and memos that my father kept. I also wonder whether it was not partly guilt about what happened that led my father to keep them. I became more sure of that when I wrote a biography of Carl Rogers, the founder of humanist psychotherapy. Rogers left over a hundred boxes of papers to the Library of Congress. Some are interesting to historians of psychology but many are trivial. Rogers even kept the bank book he had in his teens. Also, and in this he was like my father, he kept material which would show him in a bad light. Rogers' wife, for example, wrote him letters in which she accused him of being drunk, of thinking he was God, of always making love to her in the same way at the same time because it suited him. Rogers also noted his daughter warned him that he was drinking far too much.

As a lawyer and a sensible man, my father knew not just that he should not leave me alone but also that he was breaking the law. It was then, and still is now, illegal to leave children under sixteen on their own. Nevertheless, he kept records. I was in my forties when Evi, by then his second wife, gave me these boxes of papers. Some of what I have said about her may be sharp but that was how I felt when I was thirteen. Time has been a healer and I know now she did not have is easy herself. The files she handed to me included memos my father wrote to my mother. Many were accusatory and one of them, which must have been written not long after she went to Israel, made it clear that my father was very suspicious. Instead of doing her best to sell the flat, he told her, she was using delaying tactics again.

The memo is not dated and was headed 'Notes to Dolly':

1. The enclosed letter to Berg is referred for information. The fight with him will be very hard but it will be bitterly fought.
2. All other instructions given to you will remain in force.
3. We propose visiting Israel at Christmas and we hope that by then all the questions in suspense regarding the flat etc. are settled.

Note 5 offered the only concession to anything personal. My father wrote, 'David is learning very seriously and he hopes to be among the first four of his form.'

Then it was back to business: '6. You have not confirmed if you have concluded the arrangements with Asher Ben Nathan.' (He was a lawyer too.)

I wonder at what point he sensed that she would never

sell the flat even though she had gone to Israel and whether that made him care less.

Cadet Corps Woes

After my father had announced that he would be gone part of the following week, I said I was going to read in my room. I shut the door and started to cry. I wanted him to hear me, to come and talk to me, but he didn't.

As if that weren't bad enough, I had to go to school in Cadet Corps uniform on Monday and be inspected.

It was one of the ironies of public school that boys were not expected to know how to cook and clean but we were expected to know how to iron. And I had to iron my uniform. I had seen my mother ironing many times but I had no idea how to do it. I took out the ironing board on Sunday afternoon and tried to work out how to get it to stand up. Twice it collapsed under me. I took a towel out, put it on the dining-room table and rather nervously switched the iron on. I was not going to be accused of not trying. Each trouser leg got in a muddle though, and I had no clue how to put the creases in the right place. My father was reading the papers and didn't offer to help, but I don't suppose he had ironed anything in his life. After an hour I was bored stupid and it seemed to me I had creases of a sort. I had shined my shoes before so shining my boots was easier. Cleaning and polishing the green webbing of my belt and gaiters was boring but at least simple. And my shirt at least looked good because, despite the dire economic problems, we had all our laundry done by the White Knight Laundry.

On Monday morning my father said he would be home that night but home late. I hadn't told him about my trouble with the corporal so I couldn't even ask him to check very carefully that I was properly turned out. I was also scared.

If I told him I was in trouble maybe he would go away for even more of the week. I looked reasonable enough, I decided.

I got to school at 7.45. and reported to the Corps office. I had expected only the prefect to inspect me but he had called the master who had the rank of captain. Both of them looked me up and down after I saluted. I looked more like a pumpkin than a cadet, the captain said. But the British Army had a long history of drilling the incorrigible into shape. If British soldiers had been like me, Churchill would have abandoned hope and we'd all have been licking Hitler's boots, he said. Then he remembered I was Jewish.

'Not you Cohen, of course. Not that I take Hitler lightly. Terrible business but his boots were a lot cleaner than yours.'

He then told me to stand to attention while he took out a pen. 'You will take this note to your parents. Scholars are supposed to set an example in all school activities. I don't care if your Latin unseens are spot on and your history essays exemplary. I also expect you to be properly turned out and not to shamble on the parade ground like a polar bear. You're not trying. If you are not decently turned out for the next parade,' he paused to consider what punishment would be dire enough, 'you will regret it vividly.'

I quaked – did this mean there were secret floggings at the back of the school? – but only said, 'I'll do my best, sir.'

'It's an honour for a Jew to come to a school like this. Don't you forget it. You can go now.'

I remembered I had to salute again and saw him wince at my sub-Sandhurst effort.

In the afternoon, we did drill. I tried desperately hard to stand to attention, stand at ease, about turn, turn right, turn left. I was always the slowest boy on parade.

'Don't forget to show the letter to your parents,' the sergeant said when we were dismissed.

I sat on the top deck of the 73. I looked around by the time we had got to Marble Arch. There was no one from school. I took out the letter from the captain, read it and tore it up. I dumped in a litter bin as soon as I got off the bus. There was no need for my father to know I was in trouble. Next Monday I wouldn't be going to school – I had already thought about how I would manage that.

My life was changing in ways I had never expected. I had spent most of my life talking to my mother. My father lectured rather than talked. All he really wanted to know was how I was getting on at school. He might well have been scared that I would forfeit the scholarship which was worth one-third of the fees. He also wanted me to be well informed, so some evenings he would get out the atlas and discuss some of the trouble spots of the world. On some Sunday mornings he would buy all the papers, read them avidly and comment on them. But often he didn't say anything as he buried himself in the papers, his files or – his relaxation – his not so valuable stamp collection. He certainly had no interest in the things that, traditionally, bond fathers and sons together, like going to football matches. He knew that I loved and idolised him, but I don't think it mattered very much to him. Sons were there to love and admire you. It gave him no great pleasure that I did, though it would have made him furious if I did not. When I think back on it, I wonder whether, more than anything else, he just found it a burden to live with me when what he needed was the company of women or a woman.

Then, one evening, the gold standard light by which my father used to read just switched itself off. '*Pesevke*,' he swore.

'Maybe a fuse blew,' I said, though I was not quite sure what a fuse was.

My father got up and went to get the porter.

'I think you may have blown the fuse,' said the porter.

'I'd be grateful if you could fix it, Watson.'

Mr Watson, the receiver of tips and bottles of Scotch, was appalled to find there was no screwdriver in the house and went to get his set of tools.

'Living here is not possible,' my father said while he was absent. 'How can I work in these conditions?'

The porter returned with his tools and, without explaining, he turned all the power off.

'How long before you fix it?' my father asked.

'Just a few minutes, sir,' Watson replied.

When the lights came back on, my father gave Watson a pound note. Watson was properly grateful.

'I have to go Manchester tomorrow anyway,' my father said abruptly a few minutes later.

'More business with the syndicate?'

'Yes. I may have to stay there most of the week, popski.'

I did not show how upset I was.

The next morning he repeated it was quite possible he would not get back to London until Friday because the syndicate business would be very complicated. We would have Friday night together, of course. He told me to go and get a cab because he could drop me off at the bus stop before going to Euston. He kissed me fondly as the cab let me out at the 73 bus stop at Marble Arch and waved to me as he drove away.

And that was it. He never actually announced that he would be moving out but, in effect, that was what he was doing. After that Monday, he hardly spent one night at home. For a while, he kept up the fiction that he had to be in Manchester or Glasgow but eventually he dropped that. He was no longer living at home.

That Monday was significant for another reason. I had been at St Paul's for a month. There were six weeks of term to go. But I had no intention of being tortured at school by turning up for the Cadet Corps. I got off the 73 bus two stops further down at the bottom of Park Lane, crossed into Hyde Park and walked to the Edgware Road. I had worked out my plan. My father had started an account for me at the Martins Bank. I went in and took out £12. That would be enough for me to buy the cheapest possible portable typewriter.

The man in the office equipment shop was not surprised to find a young boy buying a typewriter.

I walked back to Vincent Court carrying the Olivetti. I paused on the corner by the Christian Science Church because I did not want to run into the porter, who might start asking why I was not at school.

Luckily there was no sign of Watson so I let myself in, put the typewriter on my small desk in my room and sat down. There was no reason to put up with the insufferable Mondays of the Cadet Corps. With my father not there, I would forge absentee notes. I had bought the typewriter because my father had a very distinctive flowery hand which I couldn't imitate. But if I typed the note, I would only have to forge his signature.

I practised his signature a few times till it looked as ornate as his. I smiled to myself. Then I agonised over the wording. It was best to keep it simple. 'David had a very bad cold,' I wrote, 'and so was unable to present himself for school yesterday.' I liked the word 'present', it had a certain formal feel.

I typed the words out, took a deep breath and signed. That made me nervous. Would my forgery be spotted? I typed out the note again and signed that. If I got caught, I'd be in dire trouble. But it couldn't be any worse than the Corps. The signature looked fine, I decided.

Then I settled down to read. It was safer not to go out in case I ran into Watson or a teacher from the school.

The next day, I was almost excited. I got up early, put the absentee note in an envelope and got to school early. Mr Train often sat in his classroom before assembly. I knocked on the door.

'My father wrote you this to explain why I was absent yesterday, sir,' I said.

I handed the forged note over. I was nervous again, waiting for him to spot that the signature was odd and march me straight to the High Master. I nearly blurted out the truth because I thought they wouldn't cane me if I confessed in time.

Mr Gawne, my form master, was small, swarthy and wore glasses. 'Thank you, Cohen,' he glanced at the note and filed it away. 'Are you better now?'

'Oh yes,' I smiled.

Mr Gawne told me it was a pity I had missed class because they had had a good discussion about Eliot's *Murder in the Cathedral*. I was sorry too because I liked the play, but I would have to have gone to Corps in the afternoon. If Corps had been in the morning, I might have toyed with arriving late with a note that said I had just recovered from flu – but I could hardly fall ill in the middle of the day just before parade.

I had that much common sense at least, and enough to …

1. Hide my new typewriter under my bed so my father would not find it, and
2. Only pull a sickie roughly one Monday in two.

I never found out why the school seemed not to notice that I was only ever absent on Mondays. I certainly didn't want to take any more days off. Apart from Cadet Corps, school was the best thing in my life at the time.

My father soon decided that the best routine was to have dinner together every Friday. After dinner, he would give me £20 and then put me on the number 15 bus. Where he was going he did not say. I could always get him through Mrs Brown at the office if there were an emergency.

I had become a twelve-year-old boy living alone in a luxury flat in the West End. After about two weeks, I realised this was now a permanent arrangement. Even though I had given my father my word of honour, I decided I would write to my mother. Twelve-year-olds did not live alone. I imagined that the moment she got my letter she would be horrified and book herself on the next plane to London. My mother whom I loved and who loved me would rescue me.

At the post office I asked whether there was a quicker way of sending the letter than express.

I could send a telegram, I was told. But telegrams were very expensive and I wanted to say in some detail what had happened. So I went home and wrote my mother a long letter explaining what had happened (even including the blown fuse) and how my father now hardly ever slept there. I sent it express, sure that, as I begged her, she would be back very soon.

Thirty years later, I became involved in some research on 'paracosms'. Many lonely children invent imaginary friends. It is a phenomenon recorded by the great child psychologist, Jean Piaget. Usually it happens when children are aged five to seven, but sometimes they stick to these fictions when they are much older. Paracosms are a more complicated version of this. They are imaginary worlds that children create. I was introduced to them by a very distinguished psychiatrist, Dr Stephen MacKeith. For twenty-five years he and Richard Silvey, who had been head of audience research at the BBC, collected examples of such paracosms. The Brontes had one called Gondal. Silvey died and, after he in turn had retired, MacKeith collated all their data. They had between them interviewed over thirty adults who, as children, had created such imaginary worlds. Most of these 'subjects' said they had started to make up these worlds because they were lonely and there was enormous stress in their families.

I never created such an alternative world but, alone in the flat, I did often have imaginary conversations. Well, there was no one else to talk to. I questioned God, as I have said, I talked to my absent parents and, sometimes, I explained my dilemma to the High Master of St Paul's, who, miraculously and perhaps because he was a true Christian, had never caned me. The Reverend Gilkes had made an enormous impression on me that first day when I was late.

If I presented him with the facts …

Good Lord, Cohen, I could hear the High Master say, living on your own.

With your father among the Scots.

Or, according to your mother, up to no good, forgive me being vulgar.

With your mother in the Holy Land.

Also up to no good, embezzling the family funds, according to your father.

Not very holy in the Holy Land.

The Bible does have puns, Cohen. Peter the rock.

Moses would be disappointed in your family.

I thought, being a humble Christian, that for Jews, family life was sacred, children top of the agenda.

Would you like them to do a thousand lines?

Or I could have them caned?

The caning of parents.

There would be a certain logic to it. After all, parents are supposed to bring their children up well, the High Master said in my mind. The failure of the child is the failure of the parents.

Caning the parents is the least we can do for a scholar of our school. You are a young man of promise but you must not let this family business interfere with your Latin unseens.

No High Master.

I liked reading boys' adventure stories and about the exploits of Biggles of the RAF, and so sometimes my imaginary conversations had a very Second World War feel to them.

It was hard, Wing Commander, and there were times when I wanted to top myself. I know you're a military man, sir, but I hope you understand – it isn't right, is it, for a boy to be left alone? And there were close shaves, sir, when I thought I might get caught and marched off to the orphanage. At gunpoint.

I made up these conversations with the High Master and the Wing Commander because I knew I could never tell anyone *real* the truth. I genuinely was scared that the authorities would cart me off, though probably not at gunpoint. Often I felt desperately sorry for myself, but there were also those times when I loved the secrecy. Write an essay on the following: How is it possible for a teenage boy to have mixed emotions, discuss with special reference to fear, anxiety and excitement? Marks will be deducted for self-pity.

Always, always I felt alone.

Chapter 3

The Teenager's
Survival Manual

As an adult I have written a number of self-help books,
but it has taken me till now to write the most personal
one – how to survive as an abandoned twelve- and thirteen-
year-old. There is a great of evidence to show that children
are surprisingly resilient. One of the world's great psychiatrists, Sir Michael Rutter, has studied children who were
underfed and often abused in Romanian orphanages in the
1990s. Sigmund Freud and John Bowlby would have
predicted that the psychological scars would be permanent,
but they turned out not be. Rutter found that once they
were looked after by people who cared for them properly,
over half of these appallingly abused children improved far
more than had been expected.

I had plenty of time to think in the empty flat. When I
realised that my father was not coming back, I had to learn
to do for myself things that most boys of my age never had
to bother with. So the teenager's survival manual is about
shopping, cleaning, cooking, a humane dry-cleaner and a
rabbi who should have been ashamed of himself. It is also,

and this is the hardest thing to write, about the agony of falling out of love with my mother. For a long time, I pretended to myself that she would be coming home next week and that everything would be as it had been before. But you can only lie to yourself for so long.

Poor little Oedipus, needy-pus.

Even though I had money, I had a number of disadvantages to contend with. I might be good at games, which needed hand-eye co-ordination, but I was utterly impractical. I had no idea how to fix a fuse, and even putting in a new light bulb took a bit of effort. I also had no idea how to shop, cook, clean the flat, wash or (as you've seen) iron clothes, or make sure that I was decently turned out. In the 1960s, your mother took care of all that. We didn't even have a washing machine because the kitchen at Vincent Court was so badly designed, and so, every week, my mother bundled up our dirty clothes in a big box which belonged to White Knight Laundry, a practice that my father and I had kept up. A few days later the laundry returned beautifully cleaned and pressed. I sometimes helped my mother bundle up the clothes. So I knew how that worked. If I gave the porter two shillings, he would take the box to White Knight. But a teenage boy's mind is not always focussed on laundry and sometimes I forgot. And that led to a crisis.

I was two months away from my bar mitzvah ...

The Unkind Rabbi and the Kind Dry-Cleaner

On Friday evenings I had to meet my father for dinner at 7.30 at what was now our regular venue, the Trocadero, which gave me just enough time to go to the synagogue. I found the place comforting partly because my mother loved it so much. The West London Reform Synagogue is very different from an Orthodox one. It was built in the 1840s by Victorian Jews who wanted to be as British and respectable as possible without renouncing their Judaism. The senior officers were called wardens – just like church wardens – and wore top hats as if they had paused to pray on their way to Ascot. Jews have to cover their heads but nothing in any biblical text says that they should do so in the style of an English gent on his way to a race course.

I enjoyed the service and, during the short period of silence after the sermon, I resumed my dialogue with God. I complained that He was not playing cricket with me. God, I was about to discover, did not like being put on the spot.

After the service, there was a routine. We all filed out of the synagogue into the entrance hall and stood in line to shake hands with the rabbi. The process was quick and mechanical. You wished the rabbi a good Shabbas and he wished you a good Shabbas back. I had been through the routine a hundred times with my mother. Then everyone hurried home to dinner. I waited to shake hands with the rabbi, who was in his thirties. I wished him a good Shabbas.

'How is your good mother?' the rabbi asked. This was not Dr van der Zyl, nor Hugo Gryn, but a younger man who is now dead.

'Fine, thank you.'

'Your mother is too busy cooking a nice meal to come to shul,' the Rabbi said and shook his head playfully. A mother who served up good nosh could be excused her prayers.

'Yes, my mother cooks jolly well,' I said.

'Give them my best,' he said. Then the rabbi lowered his voice. 'I want a quiet word with you, before you go home, David. Just wait behind please.' That was very unusual and I could feel myself getting anxious. I wondered what had happened. Had he discovered I was forging absentee notes? Had he guessed the truth because an angry God (who betrayed the confidences of young boys) had told him I was on my own? Logically, I knew that God probably didn't speak to the rabbi, but I wasn't feeling that logical.

When the last of the congregation had gone, the Rabbi took me aside where no one could overhear us.

'I'm glad you come to synagogue straight after school, David. It shows good intentions, but before you come you should clean up a bit. God prefers you with a clean collar. You look filthy. The Shabbas is a holy day and you desecrate it by looking like a beggar boy. I never want to see you looking like that again.'

I was not going to show one flicker of feeling. 'It'll never happen again, rabbi,' I promised.

I'm sure he thought I sounded sorry. In the future the penitent ragamuffin would only enter the House of God if he had been laundered and dry-cleaned. But I was furious. I'd make him eat his pious words. I wondered what he would say if I told him the truth.

'I forgive you this time,' the rabbi added. And then he walked away.

I ran home. If I really looked that filthy, they might not let me into the Trocadero, which was then a rather smart restaurant on Piccadilly. I stared at myself in the mirror. There was a soup stain on my tie and my shirt had a mark where some of the school mince had landed. My mother would have insisted that I put on a fresh shirt and tie before going to the service. But I hadn't noticed. That was it. I simply hadn't noticed how grubby I looked. Now I wondered whether I was being careful enough to look tidy when I went to school. I looked in the wardrobe. My shirts were decent thanks to White Knight, but now that I looked at them closely, every pair of trousers I had was filthy. My blazer told a story too – the story of all the meals I had eaten at school. It was a miracle none of the teachers or prefects had harangued me for my dishevelled appearance.

I changed quickly into the cleanest clothes I could find and hailed a cab. The driver asked me if I had the money. I showed him two pound notes.

'It is impolite to be late,' my father said.

'The traffic was terrible,' I said. I didn't mention my encounter with the rabbi.

My father wanted to know how school was, and it was easy to be honest because I was getting good marks. I told him that I had been selected to play for the Under-14s at rugby as a prop forward, which made no impression on him whatsoever. He gave me £20, told me to be careful with it and put me on the number 15 bus.

When I got home, I got out all my clothes and tried to work out which were so dirty I should take them to the dry cleaners as soon as possible. I'd never actually selected the clothes that were to go to the dry-cleaner before, and I had no idea how dirty something had to be before adults considered it *too* dirty. As I say, my mother had always taken care of that.

Better be safe, I thought. I bundled up my blazer, my Cadet Corps uniform, three pairs of trousers and all my shirts and off I went to the dry-cleaner.

Every story has a hero – and the hero of this story is Jeff Bell, the dry-cleaner. He was a small man who ran the dry-cleaner at the end of Seymour Place. He was Jewish and very friendly. I walked into his shop at nine o'clock in the morning.

'How is your mother?'

'Fine, Mr Bell.'

'I haven't seen her for a while.'

I dumped all the clothes on his table and he started to sort them out.

'My mother wondered if you could do them for today,' I said.

'Your mother knows we don't do laundry,' he said. 'Doesn't she use White Knight?'

'They didn't come this week,' I lied.

'She'll have to take them to the laundromat in Crawford Street.'

'I need my school stuff for Monday. Could she or I pick it up later?'

'I'll have the dry-cleaning ready for five,' he smiled. So I left the blazer, uniform and trousers in Jeff Bell's kind and capable hands. I headed off to learn exactly what it was you were supposed to do in the laundromat in Crawford Street.

The sign outside the laundromat was white and red. Inside it was steamy. It was pretty empty so early on a Saturday morning. A woman who must have been in her forties smiled at me because it was obvious I had no idea what to do with my shirts and knickers. 'Do you want personal service?' she asked.

'What is ... personal service?'

'It means you hand over your bag of dirty washing and you give me an extra half a crown and I do it all. And then you pick it up.'

It seemed a good deal. Even with the half-crown, the laundromat was much cheaper than White Knight, who charged between £1 and £2 a week, and I was glad of that. I had started to worry that my father would ask to see my bank book and discover that I had taken out the £12 for the

Olivetti. Now I could start replacing the money with what I saved by going to the Laundromat.

At five o'clock, I went back to the dry-cleaner.

'There you are,' Mr Bell smiled. 'Your mother's busy?'

'She's gone shopping at Selfridges. We have people coming for dinner.'

My lies were automatic now. I asked how much I owed.

'Your mother can pay next time she comes.'

'She gave me the money.'

'I was very careful with the uniform. We don't want the goys saying Jewish boys don't look spic and span.'

I would never again look like a shambolic cadet, thanks to Jeff Bell.

I wondered every time I walked into his shop if he sensed anything was wrong but he was always the same – pleasant and funny. He took pride in his work. 'No one mentioned how sharp your creases looked,' he sighed once. 'That's the trouble with my business. No one ever says, My God what a fantastic job you've done. They only open their mouths if they think it isn't clean enough or the creases don't look sharp. And you should see some of the *drek* people come in here with.' *Drek* is Yiddish for 'dirt'. 'Soup stains, egg stains, God-knows-what stains,' he laughed. Life was a matter of coping with stains.

So I got into a routine of going to his shop every Saturday morning. After a while Mr Bell stopped asking about my mother. I think he had worked out that something was wrong, but he never pressed me. Once or twice, I thought about telling him the truth, but I never did. I liked him, but how was I to know if I could trust him? I also had some sense that he might get in trouble himself if he knew I was living on my own and had told no one. The police should have been told, the 'welfare' should have been told. I didn't want him to feel that he had to involve the orphan police, who would come and take me away ...

It was the fact that Jeff Bell was reluctant to take my money which made me sure that he knew something was up. He always said that I didn't have to pay, but I always managed to in the end. To avoid suspicion.

There was one person who could have easily reported my parents to the police, school and social services – Watson, the porter at Vincent Court. My father knew that. Which is why he always gave him excellent tips and the occasional bottle of Scotch.

For different reasons it seems, as I look back, Jeff Bell and Watson both kept quiet, and I was left to cope on my own.

Gone Shopping

It would be a lie to say I had never gone shopping. My mother sometimes sent me out to buy something she had forgotten to get, and she sometimes took me shopping with her. Nearly always that meant going to Soho and visiting Camisa's for salami and cheese or Patisserie Valerie for croissants or the French butchers Randall and Aubin or Lina's Italian delicatessen. My mother got on very well with the people in these shops. They could see she was a sophisticated lady who knew the difference between a Dolcelatte and a Gorgonzola, between a filet steak and a tournedos. She sometimes asked me if I wanted a particular cheese or cake but being asked to pick a treat was very different from shopping for the basic necessities. I don't think I had ever boiled an egg.

I was not too worried about shopkeepers becoming

suspicious. In the early 1960s it was perfectly normal for children to go to the shops with a list that their mother had written. You handed the list to the grocer, he got everything the list asked for and you paid him. You didn't have to say a word.

There was a greengrocer's at the corner of Seymour Place and Upper Berkeley Street. It was run by Mr Megas the elder and Mr Megas the younger, who both wore white coats. They sold good fruit and veg and had recently acquired a large freezer.

If I had thought about it, I would have gone in with a list. But I hadn't. So I stood in the shop and made the mistake of not knowing what I wanted. Megas the elder was not a patient man. 'Look, there are other people waiting to be served,' he snapped. 'Didn't your mum tell you what to get?'

'She said I should get what I like.'

But I didn't know what to eat, and I didn't know what to buy.

'Your mum didn't give you a list?'

'No, she said it was up to me.'

He shook his bald head, muttered something about no bloody consideration and said he'd serve the next customer while I made up my mind. When he had finished, he turned to me. 'Decided what you want, young man?'

'Are those frozen dinners nice?' I asked.

'Very nice if you like that sort of thing, but I don't imagine your mum will. She's a bit fussy.'

'She'd like to try something like that,' I said.

'The beef's the best,' said Mr Megas gloomily, leading me to suppose that the lamb and the chicken were gastronomic calamities.

'I'll have one then.'

'Each packet is just for one person,' he said. 'You better

have three or you won't have enough for you, your mum and your dad.'

Safer to agree, I thought. Safer to smile like an idiot. After that I didn't dare ask for the bread, cheese, chocolate and fruit that I also wanted. It would be Delite Dinners, which were quite expensive, for three nights running.

When I walked back to Vincent Court, the porter smiled at me. 'Your dad all right up in Manchester or wherever it is he buggers off to?'

'Fine thanks,' I said, though I had not spoken to my father for twenty-four hours.

'You tell him I asked after him,' said the porter.

Yes, I thought, that way he'll feel you've earned your tip.

I was quite excited as I looked at the Delite pack. It apparently contained slices of succulent roast beef, Yorkshire pudding (which was one of the few dishes I liked at school), peas and potatoes. The instructions were simple. Place the pack in a heated oven at 400°F or gas mark 5 for twenty minutes. I had never switched an oven on, not that it was rocket science. Gingerly, as I assumed the oven might get very hot, I put the pack in. I would time it meticulously. I went back into the living room. Mr Valentin's clock – Mr Valentin was a watchmaker we had known in Geneva – said it was 5.15 and normally we ate much later, but I was ravenous. There was nothing to snack on but a Crunchie bar, and I couldn't eat chocolate before dinner.

As I waited I could hear my stomach gurgle. I was quite looking forward to roast beef and Yorkshire pudding. In another twelve minutes the Delite Dinner would be deliciousness itself. Twelve very long minutes. Ten minutes to go. Eight minutes.

I somehow kept my hands off the Crunchie bar.

Four minutes.

I was so hungry that I had to cram something into my mouth or my stomach would take leave of its senses. The pack had already been cooking for sixteen minutes, another four couldn't make such a big difference and, anyway, I liked beef underdone. Time, I decided ...

I wrapped a kitchen towel round my hand and then, just to be safe, a towel from the bathroom. Thus muffed it was quite hard to open the oven door. It was a good job I'd been careful because the moment I opened the door, a cloud of steam and smoke blasted out at me. Part of the Delite pack had turned black. I could hear my dinner bubbling inside the container. Could a Delite Dinner burp? It sounded like it. But I was so hungry I didn't care. Even through the towels, I could feel that the Delite pack was hot. I grabbed it from the oven and put it on the red Formica worktop in the kitchen.

I took out the sharpest kitchen knife and stabbed the pack open. Hot gravy splashed on my hand. I put my hand under some cold water and then I was ready for the feast.

It looked ready. And I was so hungry that I didn't even bother to sit down but shovelled the food in standing up. The two beef slices were tough, and the Yorkshire pudding and the potatoes weren't cooked. The peas were tasteless. It was more Disgusting than Deliteful, but I was starving.

I don't suppose it took me more than five minutes to eat. As I did, I couldn't but help remember the beautiful exotic food my mother made. Her cheese and spinach bureks, the aubergine salad swimming in olive oil, vine leaves filled with rice and meat the like of which I have never eaten again, and the Wiener schnitzels. All had been prepared on the red Formica worktop.

I threw the empty pack in the bin and promised myself I'd learn to cook. I would never ever eat another Delite

Dinner. If I had been a girl, my mother would have long ago initiated me into the mysteries of how to use olive oil, how to hammer an escalope so that it was wonderfully soft or how to make the dumplings for lockschen soup. But boys had their mothers to cook for them.

The next day I thought I'd be much more careful. I stopped on the way home from school at the butcher's and the grocer's. I avoided the greengrocer's: I didn't want to have to face Megas the elder again. I bought myself a rump steak, and then went to the grocer's and bought a packet of Uncle Ben's rice as well as bread, butter and cheese. Very helpfully, the packet told you to put the rice in boiling water. That was simple enough surely. I boiled some water in the kettle, poured it in a saucepan and added a cupful of rice. Then I put the steak in a frying pan. I knew I had to put in oil so I poured some oil on top of the steak. Then I turned the hotplates on. The rice started to cook but the steak was not doing its bit. It was making worrying noises, and when I tried to turn it over to fry the other side, I couldn't prise it free from the bottom of the frying pan. This lump of cow was stuck like glue. To understand what happened next, please remember that not only had I never learned how to cook, but I had never done any chemistry either. Eaton House was too mean to have a science lab and at St Paul's I was in the arts stream.

By now the steak was burning. For safety's sake, I decided, I had to pour water on the burning meat. The nearest water was cooking the rice. I picked up the saucepan and poured some of the boiling water into the frying pan. But I poured too fast. Boiling rice and water slopped on to my hand, and I spilled some water on one of the hotplates. And as the boiling water met the burning meat and hot oil there was a terrifying and completely unexpected hiss of steam.

The saucepan was in my right hand. I picked up the frying pan in my left hand. I was going to put both of them on the red Formica worktop away from the heat. But my grip was not very sure. Boiling water spilled onto my hand.

I yelled with shock and dropped the frying pan. The frying pan hit my foot and I shrieked some more. The steak plopped onto the kitchen floor.

I was off balance by now and the saucepan was tipping over. I tried to right it again but I wasn't fast enough. Boiled rice and more boiling water spilled over me.

I ran to the bathroom, poured cold water on my hands and feet and limped back to the kitchen. My dinner was now largely on the floor, which was not clean enough to eat off – I hadn't mastered the dustpan and brush either. I had to settle for bread and cheese that night. To comfort myself I spread mounds of butter on slices of the bread and ate greedily.

I went to the bathroom after I had eaten. I splashed cold water on my face to stop myself crying. I must control the tears. I looked at myself in the mirror and hated the boy I saw. My future was bleak. I was lonely, abandoned and forced to survive on bread, cheese and Crunchie bars.

I imagined what would happen if I told my father about my cooking disaster.

I burned myself, Papa, trying to cook a steak.

I'm coming home at once, you poor child.

And he would come home, horrified and guilty. He would put me to bed and feed me chocolates because I had been in danger.

And then I heard my mother's voice.

You see, you see, you betrayed me, betrayed me and

listened to your father. That's why everything you cook burns.

At certain points in life, you can go under or you can find a way to cope. I can't really explain why this kitchen calamity was a small turning point in my own life. Pride, I think. I was clever. Cleverness meant I could learn, and I knew how to learn. You learned by reading books. There were cookbooks so I would buy one. My only mistake was not go to a bookshop.

I had seen cookbooks in the local Jewish supermarket, Cohen's Smoked Salmon on the Edgware Road. It was too late to go out to buy one now but I would get one tomorrow the moment I got back from school.

'Are you sure you want this?' asked the lady at the checkout counter. 'It's very basic.'

'It's fine, thank you,' I replied. Maybe it was illegal for twelve-year-old boys to buy cookbooks.

'If *my* son gave me this I'd be offended. I'm only trying to help,' she said.

'It's not for my mother.'

'Who is it for?'

'Me.'

'What does a boy want to cook for?'

'I've got to do an essay on cooking through the ages for social history.' I was on safe ground now. She had no idea what 'social history' might mean and it impressed her.

I took the book home and studied it avidly, and I also bought a book which explained how to cook if you lived by yourself. Over the next few weeks I learned some basics of cooking – and there was only one other major disaster.

I got to grips with cooking because I was able to do it in private. But shopping continued to be a tense business because all the shopkeepers knew my mother and couldn't help but notice that they hadn't seen her for weeks. The most frightening was Mr Megas the elder. I liked to eat fruit with cheese and he always had the best fruit around Marble Arch. Every time I went into his shop he told me to say hello to my mother and that he looked forward to seeing her again. He said it with such a sneer that I almost wondered if he thought I had murdered her. (I was reading a lot of Agatha Christie at the time.) Finally he asked me if my mother was in hospital.

'Yes, it's been very hard on her.' I added that she had been operated on because of appendicitis and it had really exhausted her. Her doctors had told her that she had to rest and so she was now confined to bed. He sent me home with a big bunch of grapes as a present for her.

I kept on wondering what I could do to change the situation I was in. Every evening I did my homework, watched television, had a hot bath, which I found comforting, and then went to bed. Sometimes my father rang but not every night. And that made me pause. Had God picked on me because I was breaking kosher rules? We did not keep a kosher house because my mother loved salami so much. My father never ate it, and over the years it had been the cause of many quarrels. I loved salami and ham too, any pork as long as it was smoked. If I stopped eating pork and shellfish, would the Almighty decree that I'd had enough of a bad time? And get my parents to come back home? So I stopped eating salami in order to get God on my side again. It didn't work. In fact, God smote me with the pressure cooker.

The Pressure Cooker

My mother often used a pressure cooker, which felt like a new-fangled invention back then, but of course she had never explained how it worked. As I became more confident in my cooking, I decided that I would give it a try. I had seen her do it often enough. She poured in water, added whatever ingredients she was going to cook, closed the lid firmly and put it on one of the hotplates.

I decided to experiment on some beef, and so in went the meat, some potatoes, onions, sauerkraut and carrots. In my mother's hands, the pressure cooker had never seemed complicated or suggested it could be dangerous. I fixed the lid on tight and put the cooker on one of the hotplates.

I don't know why I decided it would take ten minutes – but I did. I went into the living room to do some homework. I didn't think I was doing anything remotely risky so I was a little surprised when I heard funny noises coming from the kitchen. I went to check and I didn't like what I saw.

The pressure cooker was hissing and steam was pouring out. The lid was no longer firmly on, and I thought the best thing was to take it off. I was a bit nervous now. Every bit as gingerly as I had approached the Delite Dinner, I picked the pressure cooker up off the heat. The lid flew off and hit me in the face. Boiling water spilled all over my hands.

This time I didn't drop anything. Though I was screaming with pain, I managed to drop the pressure cooker in the sink. My hands and face hurt. This was much worse than the steak-and-rice calamity. I turned the cold water on and splashed water on my hands and face. My hands hurt like hell. They had gone red. My face too, I imagined.

I was terrified. I thought that I must have first-degree burns. I had to get help immediately.

I ran into the street and was lucky. A cab was coming down the street. I flagged it down desperately.

'I've burned myself, I've got to go to hospital,' I yelled.

'Calm down, son,' he said. 'St George's is the nearest Accident and Emergency.'

He accelerated down Seymour Place and got me to St George's in just a few minutes. It was around seven o'clock and the traffic was light. When we got to the hospital, he wouldn't take any money and told me to go straight to reception.

I suddenly remembered that I hadn't switched the cooker off. I had visions of Vincent Court burning down. But I was too concerned about my hands and face to go back now.

Accident and Emergency was fairly empty. The receptionist called a nurse who took me into a cubicle. She put some ointment on my hands and face.

'Now how did you do scald yourself?' she asked.

The pain was not so bad now.

'I was mucking about with our pressure cooker.'

'That's a very stupid thing to do.'

'I know.' And then I added, to avoid being asked the obvious tricky question, 'My mum's playing bridge.'

'Do you want me to ring her?'

'I'm not going to have to stay in hospital, am I?'

'No,' she said. 'Are you in trouble?'

'There's a big mess in the kitchen. I've got to get home to clean it up.'

'Or your mum will go mad. It's unusual, isn't it, a boy cooking?'

'I'm doing social history for my O levels – and one of the things we study is how people have cooked through the ages.'

Social history to the rescue worked again!

'What school do you go to?' she asked.

'St Paul's. I've got a scholarship.'

'Then you must be very clever,' and she smiled. She rubbed more ointment on my face and hands. 'It shouldn't be too bad now.'

'It's much better, thank you. I just got scared.'

She smiled again and made me lie down in one of the cubicles.

Did anyone at one of London's leading hospitals ask how a well-spoken twelve-year-old boy came to burn himself and check into casualty alone? Did anyone make any follow-up inquiries? Did anyone pause to wonder whether my story was total codswallop and I was living with violent parents who scalded me?

No was the answer to all of the above.

An hour later, the nurse said I could go. She gave me a tube of ointment to take home with me.

I walked out of the hospital and felt in my pockets. I had rushed out in such a panic that I had no money and had left my keys behind. I walked up Park Lane and turned into Seymour Place. I was very relieved to see the block of flats was still standing. There had been no fire. The porter had a set of spare keys to the flat but he wasn't there.

Watson was a little surprised when I walked into one of the local pubs.

'How did you know I was here?'

'I just guessed, Mr Watson.'

I promised him a pound if he came back and let me in.

'Where have you been?' he demanded.

'I just had to go somewhere,' I said, hoping that he would not notice my bandage.

He let me in and took the pound note.

The moment Watson had gone, I rushed to the kitchen. The hotplate was glowing red. Thank God I hadn't left anything on it. I switched the hotplate off and ate bread, fruit and cheese. My father rang that night and I told him the whole story. To him, it was as if I'd come through some big adventure.

'You showed great initiative, popski,' he said. 'On Friday I will give you an extra five pounds.' Then he added, 'Are you sure you're okay?'

What will you do, Papa, if I'm not? I thought but didn't say. Dash down from Manchester or wherever you really are?

'I'm fine. It doesn't hurt so much now,' I said. I knew that my father was not going to dash down from Manchester or wherever he really was, so I'd play the part of the plucky boy hero.

The Cleaning Lady

The incident with the pressure cooker had one unfortunate effect. My father decided that it might be good for someone to cook my meals. He told me one Friday that a German lady called Anni – who knew my mother – would come to the flat to cook and do some cleaning. Anni was quite elderly, and I knew that she knew some of my mother's friends.

'I thought I'd come early to get you a nice dinner,' said Anni and smiled.

'I'm perfectly able to cook.'

'Your father is worried and thinks you need help.'

Anni thought she was doing my father a favour and she expected me to be grateful. When I wasn't, she shook her head and said, 'What manners! *Ein grobian.*' Which is German for 'a rude sod'.

'You will get used to me quickly,' Anni said.

'I don't want to get used to you.'

'I've brought you some *sachertorte* but you can't have any before we have dinner.'

'I'm not a little child,' I protested.

'I'm only doing this to help you and your parents. I don't like cooking, you know.' And she started to prepare a schnitzel – just like my mother used to do.

'I asked my father to tell you not to come.'

Anni gulped at such rudeness.

'But,' I continued, 'he didn't want to because then he would have to tell my mother.'

'I don't need the money,' Anni said. 'I agreed to do this as an act of charity – like the nuns.' All these Central European women adored nuns. Nuns did not have to worry about men, and presumably one could be visited in the convent by a good hairdresser. 'A boy like you can't clean or iron and your father is too tired to do that when he gets home late.'

So she was under the delusion that my father was still living here.

'Rudeness is not clever David,' and she unwrapped the cake, which did smell rather nice. She found a knife in the kitchen drawer and started to cut the cake.

'I don't want you or your cake here,' I shouted.

'A boy like you is too young to know what he wants. Your bad manners is because your parents have spoiled you.'

'Oh yes, spoiled me rotten. I'll never touch your food – and I don't want you here.'

'Why don't we have a slice of cake?' She smiled. 'You'll feel better.'

'I'm not going to touch your cake. If it were the last cake on earth, I wouldn't touch it.'

'I am going to tell your father how you behave. I have come here to help.'

'You are not helping.'

'If it weren't a sin to curse a child, I'd curse you.'

Anni now had a dilemma. She had been wronged – but she had unwrapped her cake. If she left it, she knew I'd eat it. But to wrap the cake up again would make her seem petty. But she was clever.

'You don't deserve the cake so I'm going to take it to the rabbi for the poor,' she said.

'There aren't many poor at the Upper Berkeley Street synagogue,' I pointed out.

'*Du kleine Schweinkind.* I will tell your father how you have been rude. And your mother. She will be so ashamed to have such a son.'

The saga with Anni did not last long. I told my father that I did not like her cooking. I would have to lump it, he said. Then I pointed out that she seemed to think he returned home very late every night. If she came regularly, she would eventually find out the truth.

'And that might be dangerous,' I added.

'Dangerous? Your mother knows already.'

'Anni is the kind of person who might report it to the authorities.'

My father paused. 'I see,' he said.

And that was the end of Anni.

I had to learn to amuse myself. Saturdays were not too bad because I played rugby and cricket for the Under-14s and later for the Under-15s at school. Sundays were harder because I was utterly alone. And if I played truant on Monday in order to miss Cadet Corps, I might not speak to anyone for forty-eight hours.

I wasn't a very original truant. I walked round the lake in

Regent's Park mainly. During one of those Monday afternoon walks, I became curious. My father had told me he was in Newcastle, where there were developments which might lead to something. I decided to take a risk. I headed for Piccadilly.

I walked across the road to Eros and sat down there for a while and considered buying a Coke. There was a burning question in mind. Was my father in Manchester as he had told me he had to be, or was he in his office in Jermyn Street, which runs off Piccadilly? I decided to walk down Jermyn Street, past the amazing cheese shop which has been selling Cheddar since 1750, past Fortnum and Mason till I got to Number 51, a few doors down from my father's office at Number 57.

Your father doesn't like being spied on because he has so much to hide, I heard my mother say.

Only now I had something to hide too. I was playing hookey.

Opposite 57 Jermyn Street and about twenty yards down a side road, there is a small alleyway. I loitered there. I just couldn't decide what to do. If I went into Number 57, and my father saw me, what could I say? That I was looking for his office, I had an urgent message for him and I'd got lost? That might work on a stranger but, of course, it wouldn't work on my father.

I waited in the alleyway.

Suddenly I saw Evi come out of the building. My father stepped out a second later.

He was no more in Newcastle than I was in Africa.

I was livid. He'd lied to me, he'd been lying to me all along. But fury was not the only thing I felt. I was relieved that he was so close. I wanted to drop all the subterfuge and go to hug him. After all, he might have come back early from Manchester.

Children are good at making lies up for their parents' benefit.

But I didn't dare. He would have hit me. So I decided to follow them as they walked out into the street. They turned into the smart arcade which gave out on Piccadilly. The arcade is narrow and I couldn't risk following them there so I went past the railings of St James's, Christopher Wren's church, and into Simpson's menswear store on Piccadilly. They were walking just like a man and woman who are together, a couple. I stayed out of sight as my father made for the Piccadilly Hotel and walked in through the grand front door.

Then I crossed the street and hovered outside the entrance to the hotel.

'What do you want, sonny?' the commissionaire in front of me barked. He was in full military regalia and sported a huge moustache.

'Nothing.' I was already backing away.

'Are you the guest or son of a guest?'

'I don't know.'

'Don't you be funny with me,' he glowered.

I just wanted to get away from there as fast as possible. I ran off past the Swan & Edgar department store at Piccadilly Circus, across the road into Shaftesbury Avenue and into the garden by St Anne's Church in Soho. As so often during this time, I was grateful for all the public gardens where you could sit and be sad and nobody disturbed you. Usually.

I realised what it was that I had been pushing to the back of mind. My father hadn't been in Scotland or Manchester. I was now sure that every time I had waited for him to call he had been with Evi. It had been going on for weeks. I suppose I had half known this all the time, but I did not want to face up to the implications of what I suspected. After all, my father always told me on Friday evenings what he had been doing in these far-flung places.

My problem was now – did I tell my mother?

Chapter 4

Writing to My Mother

I wrote to my mother eventually, but without being specific, about the date when I had witnessed my father and Evi sauntering together as a couple. Again I expected my mother to rush home. But when her next letter arrived it was short – as usual – told me to be a good boy – as usual – and made absolutely no reference to what I had told her about my father and Evi. I was baffled.

I haven't said anything till now about what was one of the most painful aspects of being home alone – the letters I wrote to my mother. I didn't say much about my cooking and dry-cleaning adventures in the letters that I wrote obsessively day after day to my mother because they didn't seem that important. What would make everything well was if I could get her to come back as soon as possible. I thought that if I could make it obvious how sad I was because she was in Israel, she would do everything she could to get back in a hurry.

As I read these letters with hindsight, with time, I am struck by how little she said when she replied to me. And I was not exactly hiding my feelings.

Monday 23rd

My very dear mother

I hope you are in good health and that my letters
give you as much pleasure as yours give me.
WRITE I BEG YOU BUT WRITE TO VINCENT
COURT.
I MISS YOU a great deal and I promise that after
the GCEs we will always be together. Luckily we
have found a cleaning woman so the house is a little
cleaner.
It is Anni.
Please WRITE because I am sad you are not here
and please send me the syllabus of the Reali School.

Lots of kisses from your son who loves you infinitely

[Here I signed it and added]

Your son who misses you so much.

The Reali School was the first school I had ever attended. It
was in Haifa. I was apparently perfectly ready to give up all
the splendours of St Paul's to go back to Israel.
My father was quite adept at working out when my
undated letters were written but this one has no date:

My dear mother

I beg you to write. I have a lot of work here.
Benjamin has gone to Aldershot for a few days where
Spitz went bankrupt. Please write to Benjamin about

the flat because I do not want to be condemned as guilty by you two. I miss you so much especially now that it is nearly my birthday. Write and look after yourself. I beg to you to take care and to take care of Safta. WRITE. I kiss you a thousand times with all my heart. WRITE. Your son who loves you so much.

The reference to Aldershot shows how poor my sense of geography – a subject I didn't do even at 'O' level – was. It takes 49 minutes to get there from Waterloo so it wouldn't have been hard for my father to get back from there at night. I wonder now what my grandmother must have thought of all this.

I would turn thirteen on 27 November. My mother rang to say that she would, of course, come back for my bar mitzvah. When a Jewish boy reaches thirteen he is old enough to be a man and is admitted as a full member of the congregation after a ceremony called the bar mitzvah. The ceremony is simple. Every Saturday morning in synagogue a portion of the Torah is read. When you are the bar mitzvah boy you read that portion. It was inconceivable that my mother would not be there, and she arrived on the Friday morning.

When I got back from school, I was overjoyed to see her. But she was not alone. She was with my Uncle Zoli and my Aunt Laura, who had come over from Paris. To celebrate they took me to the soda fountain at Fortnum and Mason.

My father and Zoli had issues relating to some business deal, and my mother thought it wiser for them not to come to dinner. My father returned to the flat on the Friday night before the ceremony. He quarrelled with my mother all evening, accusing her of not making any effort to sell the flat on Mount Carmel. On Saturday morning, we went to synagogue early. My father complained as usual that the rabbi pronounced Hebrew badly. My mother looked mortified. The rabbi responded that we were lucky my bar mitzvah had not been cancelled because I had come to so few Hebrew classes.

I had, of course, mugged up the Hebrew and read the portion of the Law without fluffing. The rabbi looked disappointed.

After the service, my father pointed out the many deficiencies in the rabbi's sermon and how he had misinterpreted the Torah. If the rabbi had ever bothered to read the Koran, he could have also explained how Muhammad, who was also a prophet, had commented on these themes.

'Barbarian,' my mother said as usual in Romanian.

My father did not come back to the flat and said we should all meet later at the Trocadero. I was desperate to have some time alone with my mother, but Zoli had never seen London and so the four of us went to look at Buckingham Palace and the Houses of Parliament. I realise now that my mother was avoiding spending too much time with me.

Usually there is a big party on the Saturday evening to celebrate the fact that the Jewish boy has become a Jewish man. Friends bring lavish gifts. But my parents had no friends and I suspect my mother insisted that Evi did not come. So there were only four guests for my celebration at the Trocadero. My Aunt Laura and my Uncle Zoli and the family dentist, Dr Shattner, and his wife. My mother disapproved of Dr Shattner's wife because, she said, she was too young for him. During dinner my father and my uncle quarrelled because my father claimed Zoli still owed him money. Zoli responded in Hungarian. My father said that Zoli knew perfectly well that he did not know Hungarian and that he would like him to repeat what he had said in a language he could understand. He was sure that whatever Zoli had said was either rude or criminal, given that Zoli was a smuggler. Zoli refused to repeat himself.

'It's a pity I can't give you pills to calm you down,' said Dr Shattner, who had cut his teeth as a dentist on my mother's family's teeth.

Then my mother explained she had to go back to Israel the next day, and she tried to make my father promise that he would bring me out for the Christmas holidays – 'if your secretaries allow you'. She smiled sweetly first at my father and then at the too young Mrs Shattner.

'Yes, we shall come to Israel,' my father said suddenly. 'You'll lend me the money Zoli, won't you?'

Everyone laughed nervously.

My father ordered some champagne and said that now that I was a man I could have a glass of claret, a glass of champagne and even a sip of cognac. I started to doze off by the end of the meal and I was fast asleep by the time we got home.

There was hardly any time to talk to my mother. As she said she would do, she took the plane back to Israel the next day. My father did not escort her to the airport. As she kissed me goodbye, she told me not to worry. We'd see each other again soon. Everything would be fine.

It was around the time of my bar mitzvah that my first term at St Paul's ended – and my shameful secret was still safe. My father kept all of my school reports. Despite everything – and in fact I sometimes wonder if it was not because of it – I had very good school reports. But then school was the only thing in my life that was really working.

Though my father had promised to travel with me, he decided at the last minute that he would not be coming to Israel. He arranged a passport for me – I was photographed in my school uniform with the silver fish that marked me out as a scholar.

According to the notes in my father's file, I flew to Israel on 27 December. Mrs Brown drove us to Heathrow and she went to have a coffee while my father took me to check in. Just before I had to go through passport control, he handed me two letters.

'They are very important, popski. Give them to your mother as soon as you arrive.'

Then he gave me a hug and waved me through to passport control. He was still there when I turned back to look and he gave me a final wave. Then I was on my own.

I was given a window seat but I wasn't interested in looking out at the clouds. I was just thinking of how wonderful it would be to be with my mother again – and to have time with her.

At Tel Aviv's Lod Airport, the passport officer looked intently at my passport. It was a British passport but she spoke to me in Hebrew.

'You were born in Israel?' she said.

'Yes.'

'And did you go to school here?'

'Yes, the Reali School.'

She then launched into a long and complicated outburst.

'I'm afraid I have forgotten a lot of my Hebrew,' I said.

'You should be ashamed,' she suddenly said in English. 'You were born here, you should be here. It's going to make me sick to stamp you in as a visitor. Do you remember enough Hebrew to understand what I've just said?' And then she asked, 'Are you an intelligent boy?'

'Yes,' I said.

'Your parents should be ashamed of themselves going abroad. We need you here to build the country,' she snarled.

In those days Israel was an idealistic country. Disgusted, the woman stamped my passport and waved me through.

The moment I saw my mother I ran towards her. She was smiling.

'Mama,' I cried.

She held me against her.

'I've missed you so much, you don't know how much I've missed you.'

'I've missed you too, *mon petit*.'

'I just hated being away from you, hated it. I tried not to show Papa, I tried not to make a fuss when you were there with Zoli and Laura, but I hated it.'

'I know, I know *mon petit*.' She stroked my cheek.

'No, you don't know,' I said fiercely.

'Well … you remember Rudi,' she said, gesturing to the man beside her.

Rudi was married to my cousin Melitta. He had witnessed some of the drama between Evi and my father's cousin Jacques. Rudi been a policeman but he had left the police and now he sold real estate. He had a slightly obsequious smile but he was no fool. And, as we shall see, he had his secrets too.

'You look very well, much bigger,' Rudi said in awkward English.

'I am.' I turned away from him and looked at my mother. 'I've missed you Mama,' I said. 'It's not much fun being at home without your mother.'

'And how is your father?'

'Fine, working hard.'

'And just where is he working?'

'I said it all in my letters – Manchester, Scotland, Aldershot.'

'Has he shouted at you a lot?'

'I mainly see him in his office or in restaurants. He doesn't shout there.'

'Expensive restaurants?' she asked.

'Sometimes.'

'Even though he's going bankrupt.' She shook her head.

I wondered if I should say that I hadn't enjoyed those dinners. 'But it wasn't the same without you.' And then it was too much for me, I wanted to be a man but I started to cry though I did not want to.

'Now, *mon petit*, no need to cry. You're here with me.'

I wiped my tears away. I didn't want to embarrass her.

'You're not a baby,' she said, 'and Rudi doesn't want to see you cry.'

'You're too old to cry,' Rudi said on cue.

My mother took out a handkerchief and gave it to me to wipe away my tears.

'*Ça va*, David, *ça va*,' she added.

'We mustn't wait here ad infinitum,' said Rudi, 'my car is parked.'

We walked to Rudi's car. My mother sat in the front with him. I was sardined into the back seat with a pile of real-estate brochures. He said he would give me some to take back to London because there were lots of rich Jews. If I sold one, he would pay me commission. He laughed.

'I'm sorry I started to cry, but you don't know how much I wanted to see you. I couldn't tell Papa because he was so busy.'

'So busy,' my mother sighed

'And I didn't want to be a nuisance. I couldn't tell the school that he had to be in Manchester, but all the time I just wanted to see you and I waited for your letters ...'

Infrequent letters, I thought but didn't say.

'Well, and here you are,' my mother said. I couldn't see if she was smiling sweetly because she had her back to me. She turned round to look at me and said softly, 'It's been hard for me too. But who was it who said I had to go, *mon petit*? I know you were only doing what your father told you to do, and it's not nice of a husband and father to force mother and son apart, but …'

'He's going broke,' I said.

'In expensive restaurants. You're a child,' she said bitterly.

'I am a child,' I said.

'Well … I've done what you and Benjamin wanted but selling the flat is not easy.'

'Oh dear.'

Was that why she had written so little, why her letters were so curt? But I didn't say a thing. I didn't want to complain in front of Rudi. I also did not want to give her my father's letters yet. I knew they would put her in a bad mood.

'We're staying at Safta's,' my mother said. 'I thought you'd be very tired.'

In London my father might gallivant with dubious women, but here my mother was his wife. Safta recognised no other women in her son's life, though she was cynical enough to suppose he was no better than other husbands. Her own husband had Casanova-ed all over the Near East, and my father's elder brother had led his wife a merry dance. But my mother was the one and only daughter-in-law. The legitimate one, Safta said. My grandmother always dressed in black like an old Arab lady. In reality she was an old Arab lady – she had been born in Morocco.

Safta's flat on the outskirts of Tel Aviv was small and rather bleak. My grandmother was a small woman with a face on which every fold of skin had been wrinkled. Her nose looked like a giant pock-marked tulip bulb. She gave me many kisses as she opened the door. She waved her arms up and down and said, in her passable French, that she was amazed how much I had grown. I never understood why grown-ups were so amazed that I had grown. The last time I had seen her I had been ten. If I hadn't grown, I'd be on the way to becoming a dwarf. Still, I knew the form. I was expected to smile and be pleased. Yes, my growth *was* amazing. Safta, for her part, seemed to be going in the opposite direction and had shrunk since I had last seen her.

Why, grandma, you look three inches shorter and you seem to have a thousand more wrinkles than you had three years ago, I thought, but did not say.

Safta and her daughter Lisa had prepared a spread. As my grandmother was an Arab Jew, Arab food was served – hummus, tabbouleh and pitta – which I always liked. I ate hungrily, which won general approval.

'You must be tired,' my mother said when we finished eating. 'I'll put you to bed.' She smoothed out the sheets in a small room at the back of the flat.

'Not really.'

'After flying all day, you must be.'

I had only flown for five hours, in fact.

'I've missed you so much,' I started to say – but then I stopped. I stopped because I knew I was going to say that I thought she did not love me any more. It seemed so babyish, and St Paul's must have begun to affect my outlook. I agree, High Master, you don't say such things out loud however bad you feel inside. Our boys didn't say they were scared when they faced the Hun.

My mother noticed the pause and took my hand. 'What is it, *mon petit?*'

'Nothing. You're right. I'm just tired.'

But it was not me speaking. It was a voice I had never expected to use when speaking to her. It was a voice I had learnt to use when I spoke to teachers, to the porter, to Megas the elder and to Jeff Bell – the voice of the boy who had something to hide.

'I told you you were tired. Where are your pyjamas?'

I hadn't packed any pyjamas.

'I'm not surprised. Your father would never think of that,' she said.

I didn't like to say that I hadn't packed any pyjamas because I had started to sleep naked. Now my father was not there, I liked to wander round the flat without any clothes on.

'We'll borrow some from Safta,' my mother said.

I had reached the ups, downs and embarrassments of puberty, and I took advantage of the fact my mother left the room to take my trousers off and get into the bed. My mother came back with some very baggy blue pyjamas.

'It's too hot to wear them,' I said

'It'll get cold in the night. Safta doesn't use much heating because Benjamin hasn't been sending her much money. You'll be sorry if you don't wear them.' She sat fussily, as mothers do, on the side of the bed. I didn't want to quarrel so I put the pyjama top on and wriggled into the trousers inside the sheet.

'You'll be nice and warm now,' she patted me affectionately. Then she smiled and bent over me to tuck me into bed. 'I'm sorry if I didn't write very much, *mon petit*. I know I didn't, but there's been so much to do and so much to worry about.'

'I know,' I said though I didn't understand. What she should have worried about was me being on my own.

She kissed me on one cheek and then on the other.

'But you're here now, so sleep well and dream beautiful dreams.'

She bent down to kiss me again. There are moments you remember for ever though I did not know that then.

But in Safta's flat I lived the first of these moments. It was neither bad nor good, more puzzling. I watched my mother bend towards me, I felt her kiss me tenderly, I saw her smile and watched her as she turned to leave the room. All sweet and maternal. But I knew precisely, perfectly why the words had not come out of my mouth a few minutes before.

Everything had changed.

It was not the same. I had spent hours thinking of the joy of being with my mother again, but now that I was here with her, it did not feel like it should.

I should have been happy, relieved, ecstatic, at home again. But I just felt cold. There was no joy, nothing was dancing in my nerves. I didn't want to think about it. It made no sense to me. My feelings seemed at a remove, so distant.

'Good night, Mama,' I said. The familiar words should have brought back the familiar feelings. But they didn't.

I felt so cold, so out of it, and I could feel the tears start up. I really did not want to blubber but I grabbed the pillow and sobbed my heart out.

I could hear the women talking in the next room. Then I heard doors slam. I had got used to sleeping alone in the flat, but here, with my mother so close, I couldn't fall asleep. I lay there, tense and quiet.

When I woke the next morning, the sun was streaming in through the window. I had to go and use the bathroom but I didn't want to get out of bed. While I lay there, I told myself that my strange reaction of the night before could all have been down to exhaustion. The moment I saw her, everything would be normal again.

'I thought I heard you wake up,' she said as she came into the room. 'I decided to spoil you.'

She was carrying a tray with croissants, cherry jam, which was my favourite, fresh orange juice and coffee.

'Thank you,' I smiled.

The smile wasn't false. But my world hadn't snapped back to normal. I felt exactly the way I had done when I fell asleep. I did not care. I could hardly believe I used to wander the streets in desperation because she wasn't in the flat and I had no idea where she was. My mother had not changed. She was being charming, she petted me, she was obviously pleased to see me, she spoiled me. She was even a little bit apologetic about not having been able to speak to me properly before and having had to come to Israel.

'Are the croissants good?'

'Very nice.' I smiled like a boy should smile when his mother is spoiling him. But the truth was horribly different. She could have disappeared, she could have been wiped off the face of the earth – and it wouldn't have mattered one bit.

'The croissant's aren't quite Valerie's but there's a good bakery quite close,' she said. She took my hand again. 'We're going to be very busy for the next few days. So many people want to see you.' She had made detailed plans. We were going to Haifa to see my Aunt Litzi, we were going to Eilat at the southern end of the Negev desert to visit my cousins on my father's side, and we were also going to Jerusalem.

'It will be wonderful while you're here,' and she smiled.

While you're here, I thought – the phrase sounded odd.

'Yes, wonderful,' I echoed.

I realised the phrase was not odd at all. 'While you're here' meant that I would go back to London alone while she would be stay in Israel. She already knew that she was not coming back with me.

I felt as if she were talking through a fog. She wasn't listening to me. She knew I had always wanted to be close to her, to touch her and be touched by her. I was Oedipal, no doubt about it. Now she was near, loving, affectionate and I didn't want her to be any of those things.

Can love die in a moment? It just had. It was a dreadful feeling.

But I knew I couldn't suddenly be rude – especially not in my grandmother's flat. So I faked it – and did it well. I had learned all about faking over the last twelve weeks. I nodded, I smiled, I said the right things. As a performance it was bloody good, or, at least, good enough for my mother not to question it for a moment. Inside I was ice. And ice that was in no mood for melting.

'You should get dressed,' my mother said.

'I will in a second,' I said.

She smiled at me and left the room.

I got dressed and remembered that I hadn't given her my father's letters.

'Papa sent me with a letter for you,' I said when I walked into the living room.

She said she would read them later. She was sure they would not contain anything pleasant.

The next few days in Israel were not awful. We went to endless family gatherings. People made a fuss of me. I played the role of the perfect clever son, and when people asked about my father, I said he was working very hard. I did not mention how much of this work forced him to go to Scotland or Manchester. They were impressed that I was at St Paul's. I smiled dutifully. One of the men I met was a lawyer who explained how hard it was to sell flats in Israel. People worried about the Arabs.

We stayed in the famously hard-to-sell flat in Haifa and I could see why my mother hated the idea of parting with it. Through the branches of the pine trees that surrounded it you could see the Mediterranean. Mount Carmel is spectacular. I wandered through the elegant Bahai Gardens where I had played as a five-year-old.

In the adventure stories I loved, the heroes never cracked. The Huns might be pointing guns at your head, the pirates might be about to throw you to the sharks, but you took it like a man.

As I lay awake at night, I promised myself I wouldn't crack. I always behaved and acted as I was supposed to. Neither she nor anyone else could have guessed my terrible secret – I no longer loved my mother.

Just a Friend

I now have to introduce a new character into this saga. At one of the dinners with my relatives in Israel, I was introduced to a man whom my mother described as 'just a friend'. His name was Mr Soussi. He was in his mid- to late sixties and he had been widowed for a number of years. He was bald, dumpy and resembled a walrus with a perspiration problem. He was always mopping his brow with his handkerchief. And even if he didn't really look like a walrus, he was by no means the suave Omar Sharif type. I didn't like him.

I mentioned earlier a picture of my grandfather with his youngest daughter leaning her head on his shoulder. It only strikes me now, as I look at the pictures of my grandfather, Alfred Cappon, and of the plump Mr Soussi, that they looked very alike. Both men had big round faces, and both were fat and had a certain bull-like blankness in the eyes. When my father had said my mother had an Electra complex, he was not wrong. Soussi was the proof of that. The Electra complex is the little girl's version of Oedipus. Electra dotes on her father.

Soussi had had some business dealings with my father,

my mother explained. He was also a millionaire.

'You must be polite to him,' she said.

'I'm always polite. I was even polite to Mr Berg,' I said.

She was encouraging Mr Soussi to lend my father some money, which might mean she wouldn't have to sell the flat. Unlike Red (and Mad) Berg, Mr Soussi was a nice man. He had suffered. He had lived most of his life in Alexandria in Egypt, where he had been a successful businessman. Then in 1956, during the Suez crisis, he, like most Jews, had fled Egypt.

'But he's a clever man,' my mother added. 'He managed to get his money out before Nasser could steal it.'

During my two weeks in Israel, I only saw Mr Soussi once. Sons are blind. I did not imagine he was a big presence in my mother's life. It never occurred to me that Mr Soussi was madly in love with her and had already asked her to leave my father so that she could marry him.

My mother knew perfectly well that if I suspected she was 'seeing' (such an anodyne phrase) another man, my whole attitude to her would change. I might also tell my father about Mr Soussi.

And there were silences and unasked questions on my side. During the whole holiday, I never asked my mother why she was not coming back with me. She never discussed it either. It was almost as if there were no point talking about it.

She knew I knew she did not dare return till the flat was sold. My father would never forgive her if she hadn't achieved her mission. And if he did not forgive, he was prone to one of his fits of uncontrollable temper.

She was often jovial but there was something odd. At some point during the two weeks I realised she was curiously uncurious. She didn't ask why I had insulted Anni, the cleaning lady. She didn't ask me many questions about school or whether I was making friends, which would have been normal for her, or whether I was going to the synagogue now that I had been bar mitzvahed.

It was only years later that I realised she felt guilty, and that her way of dealing with that guilt was to avoid asking too many questions. That made denial easier.

They taught us not to generalise at St Paul's, so I put forward this generalisation with diffidence. Children find it harder to mask their feelings than adults do. Adult life is, after all, one long mask with some moments where you show your true feelings. But I was having to learn to wear a mask all the time.

As the days passed in Israel, I continued to feel numb, angry and cold. It was as if the emotional cord between mother and son had snapped. I don't think she sensed it because I hid it – and I was determined to hide it well. But every time I smiled or was affectionate, I could always hear another voice in my head, reminding me I didn't care, and that she could die for all that it mattered to me.

As I write those lines, I'm almost shocked because, of course, they are so harsh – but it was the way I felt.

Soon the time came for Rudi to drive me back through the orange and lemon groves to Lod Airport. My mother promised she would do her best to sell the flat as soon as possible. We stood awkwardly in Departures after I had checked in. She kissed me – I let her kiss me.

'I wish I could come back with you,' she sighed.

'I have been managing,' I said.

And that was when I had so much love for you and missed you so much, I thought but did not say.

'I expect I'll manage till you get back,' I reassured her. She seemed to need reassurance suddenly.

She hugged me. I decided that it would be better to give

her a dutiful kiss too. Then she took a letter out of her handbag.

'Don't give it to your father when she's around,' she said. We both knew whom she meant. 'Wait till you're alone.'

Her instructions made me very curious about the contents of the letter.

Then I walked into Passport Control and Customs and eventually boarded the plane. In those days stewardesses used to make a great fuss of children travelling alone, but I was at an awkward age. I was far too old to be interested in crayons. Though I was in tourist class, she brought me one of the first-class lunch boxes.

'I don't know what else I can do for you,' the stewardess said and ruffled my hair.

When she touched me, it was as if I had been zapped with an electric current. Puberty meant that it took almost nothing to get my hormones racing. I watched her sashay down the aisle and wondered what I'd need to do to get a woman like that to look at me. For the rest of the flight, I tried to read a book, anything so that I didn't have to think about how I really felt to be a child who was going to be on his own again and at the same time a hormone-driven teenage boy.

How I felt about my mother could be summed up in a series of four-letter words.

Dead. Cold. Done.

'Did you enjoy your nosh?' asked the smiling stewardess.

'Yes, thanks.'

I could feel myself sweating as she took away my tray.

Mrs Brown was waiting for me at Heathrow. My father had a vital meeting he could not miss, she said, and was sorry he could not meet me. He would see me at his office in Jermyn Street. Once there, he gave me a hug and then asked me if my mother had sent a letter back with me. I handed it over. He opened it and shook his head angrily.

'You clearly did not manage to make your mother see how vital it is that she sell the flat,' he snapped.

'I did my best, Papa,' I said.

'You didn't make your mother realise the seriousness of the situation.'

I told him about the lawyer I had met who had explained that no one was buying property in Israel.

'I'm sure your mother told him to say that,' my father said. 'These Romanians are all alike. Liars. It must be the climate.' He half laughed.

I didn't know what to say.

Before I started to write this book, I always believed that the trip to Israel had brought about a total rupture in my feelings for my mother. Nothing was ever the same again. But as I look through my father's files, I begin to wonder. Memory plays tricks. Almost as soon as I got back, I was writing letters to my mother which suggest that I hadn't become quite so icy. As I re-read these letters, they seem to convey the same sense of panic and loss that I had felt before I had gone to Israel. The evidence suggests, if I try to be objective, that I did not feel so dead and cold now that I was once more separated from my mother. I started to miss her again. Previously I believed it was because I was having to cope again with the pressures of school, with the forging of absentee notes when I could no longer stand the Cadet Corps, with the whole circus of Jeff Bell, the porter, Megas the elder and Megas the younger. But today I think it is simpler. I was alone – again. I might have realised in Israel that I no longer loved my mother, but now I was alone in

Vincent Court, I missed her again. It was so much easier not to love her when she was around.

In January, two weeks after I had returned, I wrote to my mother:

> I am very sorry to have left you alone in Haifa and I am desolated to be back here alone with my father. He has not been very nice.
>
> I beg you to reply fast and I promise to go and see Lee Howard but send me his address. I decided that in the end I should come back to Israel as it is my place and Papa promised to find money to make it possible. But meanwhile I will focus on the GCEs.

Lee Howard was yet another lawyer and a friend of Zoli's. I did not know that he was supposed to gather the evidence which would prove that my father was being unfaithful. In those days, divorce law required that one party be guilty. If you could prove your husband was the guilty party, caught in flagrante, with his trousers down around his ankles, you would receive more alimony.

Men should pay for their so-called pleasures, the strudel ladies always said. Especially pleasures with the sex-retaries.

And I did not know that Lee Howard had hired a detective to follow my father, and that this sleuth was being paid for by Mr Soussi, the new man in my mother's life.

There is another letter from that time which suggests that I was not feeling as cold as I sometimes later recalled:

> My dear dear dear mother
>
> I beg you to WRITE because I miss you so much. I have just sent a packet to Shoshana and you should

have it tomorrow or Thursday. I met Edmund Barrie your hairdresser and he sent you his best wishes. He was in Haifa in October but he did not find you. I am so happy you liked the perfume I sent because I miss you so much and I beg you to write.

My usually neat handwriting had degenerated to a stressed-out scrawl.

My mother was writing no more often than she had before Christmas. And what she did write was often practical. She told me to collect some medicines from her doctor – and it was up to me to have her clothes dry-cleaned so that one of her friends, a Mrs Fechus, could take them out to Israel in late February.

Endlessly, despite everything, my mother told me I should not be sad.

And I was still trying to reassure her. I told her, for example, that new cleaners were coming instead of Anni, so that the flat would not be a total mess on the blessed day when she came back.

In a letter that I wrote to my mother on Sunday 22 March, I yet again begged her to write. I complained that my father had said he could not afford to send me out to Israel for Easter or Passover, and that the best I could hope for was that he would pay for me to go to Paris to spend part of the holidays with Aunt Laura and Uncle Zoli. They did not have the room to put me up, so I could be staying at a very cheap one-star hotel next door to the apartment block where they lived at 8 Rue de L'Etoile.

It does not require vast psychological expertise to explain what was happening to me. I had been very close to my mother. When I was six, the age when a young boy is supposed to resolve his Oedipus complex by identifying with his father, my mother left India after the incident with Miss Kaminjee and the *Times of India*. Then we lived in Israel while my father stayed in India. If my father had not been such a charismatic man, I suspect he would have found it more difficult to win back my love. When we went to Geneva, he was more present than he had ever been before and that helped to bond us, but as soon as we reached England, he became more absent again.

Children get used to new situations quickly. In those days immigrants had to learn the English ropes (more so than today). I grasped what cricket was about, learned to write English decently, and even became head boy at Eaton House. My father and mother found it much harder to adapt. He had so many illusions about Britain. Slowly, as I got some sense of British society – and I wasn't terrorised by Fat Boy Richard and Double and Quits for very long – I could see that he did not fit in. He suffered a double disadvantage. Not only was he Jewish but he was an Oriental Jew. Even non-Oriental Jews discriminate against Oriental Jews. He might have had his OBE, but my father was a stranger in a strange land. And a stranger who could not admit that to himself.

My mother tried – but not that hard. She did not really make one new friend in England. Her strudel-eating friends were all women she had known in France or Romania or Israel. But as a mother, she was (and I hope I'm choosing my words well) emotionally highly seductive. I was still very Oedipal.

I am very sceptical about Freudian theory, but I don't think you need to defer too much to the unconscious to understand why I felt so close to my mother. She was loving. She played to perfection the role of a good woman who was always being betrayed by the husband she loved. Then suddenly she was gone.

It makes me think of more words to add to the list: Depressed. Bereft. Ashamed.

Many years later, when I split up with the only Jewish woman I ever really had a serious relationship with, I came across a poem by Emily Dickinson:

After great pain, a formal feeling comes—
The Nerves sit ceremonious, like Tombs—
The stiff Heart questions was it He, that bore,
And Yesterday, or Centuries before?

The Feet, mechanical, go round—
Of Ground, or Air, or Ought—
A Wooden way
Regardless grown,
A Quartz contentment, like a stone—

This is the Hour of Lead—
Remembered, if outlived,
As Freezing persons recollect the Snow—
First—Chill—then Stupor—then the letting go—

I have no idea if critics have asked whether Dickinson was specially fascinated with metals and, as I re-read it, I think she was not that precise in her images. What is the 'wooden way' the feet go round? If it is a pier, then the next image of snow is sudden. It caught what I felt when I was thirty-five, and then I realised that Emily Dickinson had caught what I felt when I was thirteen.

One thing made my sense of loss even more acute. I was the person who had helped to persuade my mother to go to Israel in the first place.

My relationship with my father was simpler. In the love equation, I didn't love him quite so much, but I was afraid of him because he was unpredictable and, at times, violent. My mother drummed into me the fact that he was devious. Yet I didn't blame him quite so much for what had happened to me.

Ah, Oedipus. Poor rejected Oedipus.

After I came back from that shattering trip to Israel, my parents seemed less and less able to communicate with each other. Both wanted me on their side and so, without realising what I was doing or what it would lead to, I started to negotiate between them. In June that year I wrote to my father. The letter suggests that he wanted us to move to a new and less expensive flat.

> The fact that I agreed to leave is not a reason to browbeat my mother and bombard her with letters. Reason is all very well but the sort of pressure you are pulling on appears to be tantamount to childish hysteria. You must give time for us to find a new flat. I'm not taking anyone's side but I would prefer to see my parents behave like civilised people – be they Semitic or Balkanic – I hope you don't find such language too strong but you have always taught me that honour, truth, decency and moderation are the basis of a man's life.

I signed it, 'your devoted son'.

Many of these letters are repetitive and there is no point in quoting them more. And even as I was writing such letters, I managed reasonably well at school. No one guessed that I was living on my own or that I was forging absentee notes. I made it into the Under-15 cricket team though I was not good enough to open the batting as I had at Eaton House. Academically I did well. I sat my O levels in the summer and got nine, including Additional Maths. My father was pleased by my school reports and the acute crisis with Mr Berg had somehow passed.

When he became famous and ran the psychology department at Johns Hopkins in Baltimore, one of my intellectual 'heroes', the psychologist John B. Watson suggested that anyone who wanted to work as a psychologist should first analyse his strengths and weaknesses. To enable people to do so, he devised what he called the Balance Sheet of the Self.

I liked this concept the moment I discovered it because it makes thinking about yourself less a matter of convoluted introspection. The Balance Sheet is really a list of good and bad.

I like to imagine how I might have filled it in when I was thirteen.

My weaknesses:

- I felt abandoned by my parents
- I felt angry with my parents
- I was perplexed by the sense of deadness towards my mother
- I still did not know how to drill for the Cadet Corps
- I was often anxious for no reason
- I still sometimes dissolved in tears
- I had no friends at school

My strengths:

- I was coping with all my school work
- I had not broken down under considerable emotional pressure
- I had learned to cook
- I had learned how to shop

- I was not frightened to sleep by myself in the flat
- I could manage money perfectly well (my father's £20 was a very generous allowance but I never ran short)

In his balance sheet, Watson did not allow for ambiguities. But I am certainly aware of them now:

- I had stopped dreaming (to this day I rarely remember my dreams)
- I often felt quite emotionally dead
- I had become good at forging letters (a useful skill but not an admirable one)
- I had become good at lying (again this is hardly admirable, but if I had not become good at pretending, lying, ducking and diving and dissembling, so that the grown-ups had the wool pulled over their eyes, I'd never have survived)

Of course, these are not skills that your school, your parents or any grown-ups are likely to tell you that you need to develop. But I can imagine the report ...

Lying – Cohen has made excellent progress in telling fibs and should achieve top marks in dissimulation.

Forgery – unfortunately Cohen has not paid sufficient attention to his Ps and Qs, which look as if they were far too hurried. The good forger needs more patience than he seems to have.

General – Cohen will have to buck up his dissimulation if he is to get the scholarship to the University of Fraud that we all think he can achieve.

There was nothing nearly as interesting in my real school reports, which my father kept. I found a note in one that said the High Master had been unable to add his usual comments because he had had a bad bout of influenza.

Chapter 5

The Delights of Deception

Today social services are often criticised for failing children in need. It often sounds as if in the less complex society of the 1950s and 1960s, the needs of children were met. I doubt it, given what happened to me. I feel through the cracks.

Children in despair sometimes are silent out of shame or fear but, sometimes, the real problem is that no one pays any attention when they do cry for help. When I uttered 'cries for help', as the psychobabble calls them, no one took a blind bit of notice. I might as well have been an elephant yodelling on the moon. Presented with clear signs that suggested a boy was in some distress, teachers, nurses, family friends and the local rabbinate didn't ask a single question which could have led to the truth. No one queried, for example, why I was absent for school so often. And it was not just the authorities who were blind. My aunt and uncle in Paris knew but did not lift a finger to help.

I could, of course, have gone to the High Master of St

Paul's or to the rabbi and explained the truth. I didn't, but I sometimes wonder what would have happened if I had.

The High Master shook his head.

Oh dear, oh dear, Cohen, you are sure?

Yes, sir, I am sure my father does not live at home.

I suppose I shall have to ask him why.

His mistress, sir. He lives with his mistress.

Are you sure? Jews don't do that sort of thing, do they?

King David had concubines, sir.

Yes, about eight hundred of them if the Bible can be believed and, as I am a clergyman, I do believe, boy.

I knew I had to keep up the pretence that I was living a normal life with my parents at home. I told myself I was being very clever, learning to cook, doing the dry-cleaning and having the laundry done. I struggled to make sure I did not look like a tramp when I went to school. This has left its mark on me, and I somehow resent having to look decently turned out even today. It's as if being smart were somehow not to be true to myself. Silly, of course, but a real feeling nonetheless.

My father did not know anything about social services but he was frightened that someone would find out what was going on. He kept on bribing the porter, and I suspect that Anni was also given a series of lavish tips to make sure that she did not blab. But then my father was a gambler, and I think he had reached a desperate time in his own life.

I was soon to learn that even the most unlikely people were capable of deception.

Thanks to Jeff Bell, my Cadet Corp uniform looked smart enough. I really did not want to get into trouble so I spent quite a lot of time polishing my boots and blancoing my gaiters, but despite all that I did not look very military on those Monday afternoons when I did turn up to school. And my parade ground skills were still zero. I slouched and I was always slightly late when we had to turn left or right. I also found myself marching out of step with all my fellows. I hated drill.

'You're bloody useless,' the sergeant would yell.

Major Retallack, who was the Commanding Officer, disliked me. One reason was that I had become involved in the school play, Moliere's *The Miser*. I had a tiny part, acted as the prompter and understudied the lead. As far as Retallack was concerned, I had no business doing anything other than school work if I was such a useless soldier. I was, he told me, probably the worst boy cadet he had ever seen and since I was not a halfwit, it showed that I didn't care.

'Who do you think saved the Jews from Hitler, boy?' he barked. It was the lads from the Cadet Corps apparently.

The Cadet Corps fiasco came to a head when they put a rifle in my hands. I was even worse at shooting than I was at drilling. I was possibly the worst shot ever on the shooting gallery of St Paul's.

Though I hated the Cadet Corps I did not want to be a total failure. And so I hoped that when we went to the army shooting range at Bisley I would not make a complete idiot of myself, even if I didn't imagine I would hit fifteen bull's-eyes. We had been taught how take a gun to bits, clean it and reassemble it. I just about could manage to do these things, but once Private Cadet Cohen had a rifle in his hands, mayhem would ensue. I realise now that the reason is simple. I have a strange congenital defect. I can close my right eye and leave my left eye open, but I can't close my left eye and leave my right eye open. We were being taught to shoot with our right eyes open.

I was tense as we lined up in front of the targets. I yanked the rifle up to my shoulder and nestled it between my blades. I tried to take aim. And here was the problem. As I shut my left eye, my right eye wanted to shut too. I couldn't see the bloody target properly.

Retallack told us we had to relax, aim and fire. I was about as relaxed as if I had been put in a cage with a hungry leopard. I suddenly felt I had no control over my muscles at all. When the sergeant yelled, 'Fire,' my rifle suddenly pointed upwards but I still pressed the trigger. I did not hit the target.

Oh no.

I hit the flag that fluttered above it. Everyone laughed.

Retallack came over to me and took the rifle out of my hands. He said that I was either taking the mickey or a dangerous lunatic. If he could have had me court martialled, he would have, I'm sure.

Naturally, the other boys made fun of me. It was the talk of the coach as we drove back to Hammersmith. When we reached the school, Retallack came over to me.

'I want a word with you,' he barked, 'in private.'

I followed him into his office, and he shut the door.

'Stand up straight, boy. Do you want Monty to have a heart attack?'

'No sir,' I said, though I wasn't sure how I would give the victor of El Alamein a coronary.

Field Marshal Montgomery would be coming to inspect the Corps. Major Retallack had no intention of insulting the Old Pauline who had won the Second World War by forcing him to watch me march out of step.

'The best thing might be if you stayed out of the way,' Retallack said.

'But, sir ...' I was careful not to protest too much.

'You might have to have a bout of flu or something. Do you understand what I mean?'

It was too good an opportunity to miss. 'You want me to pretend to be sick so I don't muck up the drill?'

'I've never done anything like this,' Retallack went beetroot red with shame.

So the situation was that I, who had truanted so often – and forged absentee notes – was being told by my teacher and superior officer to play truant. For the good of the regiment, the school and the continued beating of Field Marshal Montgomery's heart.

'I will be very disappointed, sir.'

'The man did not win the Second World War to be confronted by your shambolic drilling,' Retallack shouted.

'If it will help, sir, I will do as you say.'

I smiled, deferential, glad to be of use and, of course, I knew that it would be very hard for Retallack to ever question my absentee notes.

'Help? *Help?* Nothing will help you, Cohen,' Retallack said.

I did not write to my mother to explain what had happened and I had no intention of telling Dr Benjamin Cohen OBE that his son had been told to go absent without leave by the Commanding Officer.

Psychology tells us children feel powerless when their parents quarrel. I was in a very paradoxical situation, however. On the one hand, I really was powerless, an abandoned child. On the other hand, I was taking some control partly by playing truant and following my father, and partly by continuing to do well at school. I was now an expert on the causes of the Reformation, King Lear, the wives of Henry VIII, the poetry of Thomas Hardy, how British privateers explored the world in the sixteenth century, *Much Ado About Nothing* and anything else you might need to know in order to do well in your exams. I was good because I swotted. If my work was good, St Paul's would have less reason to be suspicious.

But I had two secret ambitions. I had played Falstaff in the school play at Eaton House and I had become involved in the school play during my first term at St Paul's. I had started to write a play of my own. I had visions of myself as an actor and playwright.

My second ambition was to kiss a girl. That seemed like a fantastic dream.

It's easy to forget how different the 1960s were when it came to sex. It was not so much dirty but secret. Pre-teen girls did not read magazines which told them how to make themselves up, what they could expect of boys and about contraception. In 1961, Douglas Price and a number of actors made a brave film called *Victim* which dramatised the case for homosexual law reform. The 1889 Act which outlawed sex between males was still being enforced, and young policemen often went into public lavatories in the hope of getting men to proposition them so that they could be arrested. The age of heterosexual consent was eighteen. The contraceptive pill was not yet an unremarkable fact of everyday life. Ken Tynan had not said 'fuck' on television.

It was another world, a pre-modern, pre-permissive, pre-everything-we-take-for-granted-now world, and I was trying to grow up in it. There is no doubt that I was lonely and emotionally confused. I know now that emotional confusion leads teenagers into trouble.

I couldn't shake off the idea that somehow I was to blame for my predicament. I had gone through puberty with one great disadvantage. Because I lived alone, I couldn't make life hell for my parents, of course, and I missed them. When it came to sex, I was more confused than I liked to admit or even than I realised. In theory it was simple. I fancied girls. All my fantasies were about girls.

My only brush with anything not hetero (not that I would have used such terms at the time) was a crush I had briefly on another boy at school. He seemed very self-assured, which may have been due to the fact that both his parents were psychiatrists. William, who in later life became a spiritual preacher, used to make authoritative pronouncements. Nothing ever happened, of course.

Most of the events described in this book gave rise to feelings that I can remember fairly precisely and I can try to explain them – but not this. Freud would have said I was repressing my feelings because I didn't dare admit I had homosexual impulses. Freud was ambivalent about homosexuality. It was a perversion but he allowed his biographer Ernest John to suggest that there was a homoerotic element in Freud's relationship to Carl Jung who for ten years he saw as his heir. Freud claimed homosexuality was often the result of a boy's identifying too closely with his mother. Normally, a young boy realises at the end of his Oedipal stage that he cannot kill his dad and sleep with his mum. To make the disappointment bearable, young Oedipus, aged six to seven years old, switches loyalty. He stops being so much of a mummy's boy and starts to worship his father and identify with him. Father and son often bond and band together. Of course, young Oedipus is not consciously aware of any of this, but it is all bubbling away in his sub-pre-unconscious.

One evening, not long after I had turned thirteen, I set off on one of the long walks I took when I could no longer bear being alone in the flat. I headed towards Hyde Park and decided, for no particular reason, to go down the Bayswater Road. I got to Queensway and walked down that. I looked around at the busy street – there was a folk club just by the Tube but I didn't dare go in. I was stood looking at it when a car drew up and hooted.

I had no idea that the road was nicknamed Queersway then.

The driver smiled at me. He was a thin middle-aged man wearing a sports jacket. He could have been one of my teachers. 'Fancy a lift?' he asked.

When I think of what I did next, I am surprised. Perhaps it was the fact that he seemed so familiar, so teacher-like, that made him unthreatening.

'Yes,' I said.

He asked me where I was going.

'I'm going home.'

'Hop in and I'll take you,' he said. It would be great if he could drop me off near Marble Arch, I said. I sat in the front seat. He told me his name was Turnbull. He added that when he had been at school, he had been good at sports. I looked like I was good at sports, he smiled.

I did play at prop forward for my school, I said. He was very impressed when I told him I went to St Paul's.

Did I like rugby? he asked.

'Yes.'

Did I like all that mucking around in the scrum?

'As long as it isn't too rough,' I said.

He asked me my name. When I said it was David Cohen, he grinned. 'Your race is usually known for its brains rather than its bodies.' And then, after a pause, 'I suppose you're circumcised.'

'You have to be if you're Jewish.'

'But there's nothing wrong with that. The Covenant with the Lord and all that.'

We had stopped at the traffic lights by Lancaster Gate

Tube. As we stopped, he took his hand off the steering wheel and very gently placed it on my knee. It was a complete surprise. No one had ever done anything like that before. 'Would you like to have a drink at my house?' he asked.

I was too embarrassed to say anything.

'But some Jews like you seem to have, I bet, a very beautiful body.'

'I don't know.'

The traffic lights changed to green. Turnbull took his hand off my thigh and back on the steering wheel. He drove slowly. By the time we had crawled to the next traffic lights, they were red. Again he put his hand on my knee.

'There's nothing to be scared of. It's fun.'

I was on edge. I didn't like his hand there.

'Could you please stop and let me out,' I said.

'Why were you thumbing a ride then?'

'I wasn't,' I insisted.

'Don't lie, young man.'

'You offered me a lift home.'

He laughed, not unkindly, which I found scariest of all. 'You can't be that stupid.' And then he paused. 'We all want love.'

I realised I was in trouble. I put on my head boy's voice. 'Please stop the car and let me get out.'

'You'll get out when I let you,' he said sharply.

But Turnbull wasn't much of a monster. His only revenge was to drive me past Marble Arch and down to Hyde Park Corner, where he told me to get out. 'You shouldn't tease people or you'll get into real trouble. You're lucky I'm a nice man. Get out now,' he said. I got out fast and slammed the door. 'Take my advice and don't tease people, you little prick.' He accelerated away.

Ironically, he had left me fifty yards from St George's Hospital, where I had come after the pressure-cooker drama. I didn't fancy risking the walk along Park Lane. So I waited for a bus to take me back to Marble Arch.

Being picked up once might be an accident, but, as I look back, I see that I kept on inviting it. I found myself asked by men to go for drinks, to go sailing, to go to clubs. This was very strange since all my fantasies were to do with girls. I realise now that I was obviously sexually ambivalent but at the time I saw myself as innocent.

Even if I had had a better relationship with my father, I would not have talked to him about any of this because it was too embarrassing. But, of course, my relationship with my father was fraught and episodic. And he would go berserk if he had any idea I was putting myself in dubious situations with men.

A few weeks after I had escaped Turnbull, I left the flat for another evening walk. I could have turned left at Marble Arch and gone down Oxford Street but at the Cumberland Hotel I turned right. Yet again I was walking down the Bayswater Road towards Queersway. I was a little excited and a little worried. Twice cars slowed down and offered me lifts. London seemed full of men who cruised slowly in their cars, waiting to pick up boys who should have known better. Well, I wouldn't get into anyone's car. I had reached Notting Hill now. Maybe it would be smarter to go to the cinema than walk around these dangerous streets.

At the local cinema there was a French movie with a 15 certificate. I went up to the box office.

'You don't look fifteen,' Box Office decreed. 'What year were you born?'

'1945,' I fibbed.

'Can you prove it?'

Of course I couldn't. But there couldn't be much in the film that would shock the West End Waif, so I thought I'd act clever. 'I don't shock easily.'

'Seen it all have you?' said a friendly voice behind me.

The man with the voice whispered in my ear. 'I'll tell you what. I'll be your long-lost uncle who works on the P&O.' He introduced himself as Tickie. He was in his thirties and had a very upper-class accent. He was tall and his blond hair was brushed back. He wore quite a smart suit. 'You haven't run away from home?' he asked impishly.

'No, I haven't,' I said, and I handed him the money for my ticket.

'Uncle's treat,' Tickie said. 'The brat's with me and he *is* fifteen. He's my nephew.'

That was good enough for Box Office.

'I didn't mean you to pay for me,' I said once we had our tickets and were in the foyer.

'Why don't you buy us some choc ices? Then we'll be square.'

We? Would that mean we would be sitting together in the dark? I did as I was told and bought us each a choc ice.

As the lights went down I remembered Thighs Turnbull. Was Uncle Tickie going to be the second man to put his hand on my knee? Was that why he had been so nice? But Tickie just bit into his choc ice and concentrated on the screen.

'I love the ads,' he said.

I got lost in the movie. For a little while I was tense, expecting Tickie to try to touch me. But he never did. He didn't so much as brush my knee, shoulder or thigh. But maybe, I thought, he was being clever. He was waiting till it was all over and then …

The smart thing would to slip out while the credits were still rolling. The moment the first credit appeared, I stood up and made my way brusquely past all the people sat in our row. I heard them mutter that I was being rude. I had just walked out into the foyer and was making for the exit when I felt a hand on my shoulder.

'That wasn't very polite of you to leave without saying goodbye,' Tickie ticked me off.

'I have to get home,' I said.

'It's still rude. Anyway, I'll give you a lift.'

'I don't want a lift,' I snapped, and then remembered my manners. 'No thank you.'

'I don't eat little boys who lie about their age,' said Tickie and smiled. He looked so friendly that I felt guilty. Most men were not queers, after all. Most men had the kind of dreams about girls that I had.

'What do you think I'm going to do?'

'I don't know,' I said, embarrassed. It was true. I had no idea. The game we had played at Eaton House with our school caps, trying to hit each other's genitals, was the closest thing to sex with anyone else I had ever been involved in.

'Well, I'll be your chauffeur then.'

I sat on the front seat of his flashy sports car, tense at the thought of a stray hand, but nothing strayed my way.

'It's only ten. Come and have a look at my telescopes.'

'My dad's expecting me,' I lied.

'Where's your mum?'

'In hospital.'

'I'm sorry to hear that.'

'I shouldn't stay out late.'

Tickie looked at me curiously. I realised later that he had twigged something was not right. Middle-class boys did not

go out on their own on a week night. But he didn't say
anything.

'If you're too good, you'll never have fun in your life.
Swots have awful lives.'

I wondered how he had guessed I was a swot and that I
was not having much fun in my life.

We drove fast down Park Lane and stopped in Knightsbridge near the back of Harrods. We went up into a red-
brick mansion block. His flat was on the fifth floor. When
he opened the door, I entered into a world that was like
nothing I had ever seen. The walls were hung with modern
paintings and old red tapestries. There was an amazing
collection of scientific instruments, an old globe, three telescopes, a sextant.

'Do you know what that is?'

'A sextant,' I said.

'The child has depths.'

One of my special papers for history A level was on the
expansion of Europe. I knew more than any thirteen-year-
old should about the politics of pepper, the wars caused by
ginger and how sixteenth-century sailors worked out their
latitude. Tickie patted me on the shoulder and invited me
to peer through the telescope.

'Do you like my instruments?'

'They're amazing.'

'I keep some more in the bedroom.'

I was not going to go into his bedroom.

'But I'm not going to show those to you now. I like my
telescopes. Very phallic if you know what that means –
which I suspect you do.'

'I know.'

'You must be advanced for your age.' Tickie put on some
classical music and sat down on the carpet. 'You're not shy

about drinking are you?' He got up again and returned with a bottle of red wine, two glasses, some Bath Oliver biscuits (which I had never had before) and some stilton cheese. 'I'll throw you out if you say you prefer Coke.'

'I hate Coke. I like Châteauneuf du Pape.'

'The child is unbearably pretentious,' said Tickie, shaking his head. He sat down again on the carpet and, this time, he was much closer to me.

I tensed and quickly got to my feet.

'Do sit down, silly child. Nothing will happen that you don't want to happen. You've been here before, haven't you?'

'I've never been in your flat.'

'I meant in this kind of situation.'

'No,' I said.

'I'm good at spotting liars, child, being a bloody good one myself.'

I felt embarrassed now. It was a little like being in Turnbull's car, but Tickie was still not trying to touch me.

'You're a tense little soul,' he said and yanked himself up. He sat down on the sofa behind me. Suddenly I felt a hand on my shoulder. 'There's a lot of tension in these teenage shoulders.'

'No, there isn't,' I said, but I didn't push his hand away.

Tickie began to rub my shoulders gently. 'Is that nice?'

It was nice. No one had ever rubbed my shoulders before. Shoulders were not knees, shoulders were not thighs. It was perfectly kosher to be touched so far from the bits that mattered.

'Sip more wine. There are few pleasures to compare with having your shoulders massaged while you have a nice drink. I'm sorry this is not a Châteauneuf du Pape. I'll get one for next time.'

I have no idea how long he continued to rub my shoulder. He did nothing else and then, rather suddenly, said, 'I better drive you home or you'll be in the shit with your mum and dad.'

I wanted to ask him how he had worked that out. He drove fast up Knightsbridge and to Marble Arch. As he drove, I was worried that if I let him see where I lived, he would notice that all the lights were off and realise I was living alone.

As the car slowed down, a policeman was walking past the entrance to Vincent Court.

'I better drop you at your front door or that policeman might ask questions,' Tickie said. 'You don't want to be interrogated when there isn't anyone at home.'

'How do you know that?'

'There isn't one light on in the block.'

'Oh yes.' I had no idea that all the other people in Vincent Court went to bed so early. Luckily Tickie was able to explain the darkness.

'Mum in hospital, dad gone down to the pub … No, your father's not the pub type because he must have taught you about Châteauneuf du Pape. I don't mean to be rude but let me guess … Dad is the Casanova type. Unless – what a delightful thought – he plays both sides. Probably not. So while your mother is in hospital, your dad is canoodling with a secretary and comes back way past midnight. Am I right?'

He paused for a second. Then he added 'My dad used to do that. Broke my mother's heart.'

When I heard that, I was an inch from telling him the truth, but I stopped myself.

The policeman turned into the next street.

I was about to say thanks for having me, but he hadn't. 'I enjoyed myself. Thanks.'

'Why don't we go see a film Saturday? There's a Bergman on and you won't get in without your uncle. I'll be at Notting Hill tube at 7 p.m.'

'I'm not sure.'

'We'll have fun like tonight,' he said casually, 'but suit yourself.'

He drove off. Quickly, before the policeman reappeared, I let myself into the silent flat.

All week I couldn't decide whether to meet Tickie or not. But I'd spent all Saturday on my own. I was bored so by 6.15 that I took a bus down to Notting Hill. He was there with a big smile.

'So you decided I wasn't a monster.'

He bought the tickets, and I bought the sweets.

We watched the movie, which was extremely gloomy. As the lights rose I didn't try to flee as I'd done the last time. Tickie said we should go and have a drink.

I could have said goodbye at the end of the movie. I had the money to take a cab home. Or the 88 and 12 buses would get me to Marble Arch. So would the Central Line.

Tickie knew better than to be too pushy. Casually, he said, 'I've got some Châteauneuf du Pape in. Good year too.'

'I ...'

'Are you or are you not interested in wine, child?'

We got back to his flat. He brought out the bottle with some ceremony. For a while we talked about the movie and then he smiled.

'How are the tense shoulders?'

'Fine.'

'Don't believe it, shoulders always need a rub. I have yet to encounter a shoulder that didn't say yum-yum when someone offered it a rub. In fact, my shoulders need a rub.'

He placed himself on the sofa. It was obvious what I had

to do. Giving someone a massage was hardly that intimate, and he'd done it to me. I started to rub his shoulders. He made a few appreciative noises but he didn't suddenly go sex-berserk.

'You've got good hands,' he said finally.

'Thanks,' I said, not knowing what else to say.

'I shall now return the compliment,' he said and flexed his hands.

At first it was just like it had been earlier. Nice but distant.

'You need a proper back rub, young man.'

'I'm not sure,' I said a little anxiously.

'Lie down, there's no harm in a back rub,' Tickie said softly.

He didn't say a word as he rubbed my back. He had put some Bach on. At first he rubbed my back through my shirt, but then he put his hands inside it. I became conscious of the fact that I was getting an erection, which puzzled me. He was a man and all my fantasies were about girls.

'Now you are going to be like a compass.' He spread my arms out east and west. 'You are a scientific instrument. I expect you've learned about compasses at school.'

'The Vikings had a primitive compass,' I informed him, 'but it was perfected by the Italians so that when Columbus headed for America he knew where he was going.'

'You are mine,' he said. 'A mine of information. Just my little joke.'

Being a compass was very relaxing. I was still half expecting him to do something else, something I knew was bad, wrong, not kosher. But all Tickie did was stretch my legs out. 'This leg is the south-east,' Tickie repeated. 'South-east, south-east, south-east.' He massaged my leg down to the ankle. 'Now that leg is much less tense.'

He opened a second bottle and poured us another glass each. The mood changed only slowly, and his massage became more of a caress.

'I see we have a bulge,' said Tickie and smiled. 'Jolly good.'

By now I was a little drunk.

'Shall I feel if we have a bulge,' he said, and before I could reply, he was feeling it.

'Please don't.' I was suddenly tense. I squirmed away. 'I don't want you to do that. You said that nothing would happen that I didn't want to happen.'

'But you do want it to happen. Your problem is that you don't know that you do. After all, why did you come here tonight?'

'To see a Bergman movie.'

'And we're in the movies now, are we?' he laughed.

I heard the sound of his zip being undone. I got up fast.

'Is that how you want it, you little bugger,' he smiled.

'Look, I'm really sorry, but my father would never forgive me.'

'Casanova Cohen, the perfect pa.'

It totally threw me when he used the same words my mother did so often.

'Your father's out with his mistress, and I bet you're only playing hard to get now. I used to play hard to get when I was a boy, but I always got got in the end. Shall I chase you round the sofa?'

'I'm not queer,' I snapped.

'Don't use that nasty word and, by the way, let us look at the evidence.' He stopped suddenly. 'If you weren't queer or half queer or quarter queer, your prick wouldn't be hard as a rock and standing to attention waiting to be saluted. I salute your prick.'

He laughed at his mock salute.

'Please leave me alone,' I said.

Tickie had a moment of conscience. 'Don't tell me you've never done this before.'

'No.'

'Not even with your mates in the showers?'

'No.'

'Standards must have fallen at St Paul's,' he laughed. Then he came close to me. 'Look, we like each other. I promise I'll be very gentle. You got me so excited because you are very lovely and, I'll admit it, so young.'

'I must go home.' I edged towards the door.

Suddenly he looked sad. 'You mustn't leave me like this. It's not fair.'

'Fair?'

'I'm all worked up, all systems go. Anyway, you'll love it. I give you my word as a gentleman.'

'I don't think I will love it,' I said. And then I had a shock. I had never before seen what desire could do. Tickie had seemed a nice man, a kind man, a rational man. The thing to do was to keep cool and keep talking. I was moving towards the door. I wasn't sure what kind of crisis this was, but if Biggles had ever been in one like this, he had not written about it. Face the enemy. I turned round slowly and coolly.

Tickie's penis now struck out of his pants like a large carrot.

'You really shouldn't have come back here if you didn't want to do it,' he said. 'It's not fair on a bloke.'

'I didn't know ... I'm just thirteen.'

'And innocent as a daisy. Don't pull that one. You were looking for something. Not enough mummy love, not enough daddy love.'

That made me pause. Did I show it so obviously?

And in the pause, he caught up with me, grabbed me from behind and put his hands on my prick. He was pressing himself time and time again against me and letting out a series of yelps. 'It's fantastic,' Tickie cried. 'Don't you love that?'

I didn't know what to say. Tickie sounded like he might be having a heart attack. His breathing got more and more frantic. Then suddenly he calmed down. He was his old self again.

'You came. Did you know that?'

I could feel the wet in my pants. I felt relieved and I also felt like crying, though I didn't really know why.

'It was lovely,' he smiled. He was calm again. 'Won't you have a glass of Châteauneuf du Pape?'

'I'd just like to go,' I said unsteadily.

'I can't let you go like that. You've got spunk on the back of your jeans and the front too because, my little friend who says he's not queer, you came like a fountain. Gushing spunk,' he laughed. 'You'll find out it tastes salty.'

'It doesn't matter.' I just wanted to get out now.

'Don't worry, I've got just the thing if you don't want to get home with an embarrassing spot on the front. Mothers notice these things. My father beat me to a pulp when he found out.' Tickie rummaged in one of his chests of drawers and got a spatula. Then he dashed into the kitchen and came back with some Dabitoff, the instant dry-cleaner. He scraped the spunk off and dabbed my trousers with the fluid. He patted the stain. Then Tickie stood back and examined my trousers.

'You look decent,' he said. 'No one will guess you've been up to less than I hoped.'

I was shaking like a leaf, shaking because I hadn't expected it to happen, shaking because I felt he'd done something violent to me but also because this was the first time someone had made me come.

'You can stay you know. We can do it better,' he smiled.

I shook my head.

'Well, I'm sorry, but at least you look respectable now,' he smiled. 'Do you need money for a cab?'

'No need, I've got enough.'

I was at the door now. 'Thank you ... for ...' I stumbled.

'I believe at your age boys still say thank you for having me,' he smiled.

I was out of the door and running down the stairs. I didn't stop running till I was fifty yards from the his block of flats. The air felt sharp and good. I'd drunk too much. I expected him to rush out behind me but he didn't.

Finally I saw a cab and hailed it.

'Aren't you out a bit late, son?'

'I've been visiting my crippled aunt. She likes me to read to her till she drops off.' I hoped I didn't smell of wine, Dabitoff or spunk.

'It's past midnight,' he said. 'How old are you?'

'Auntie just couldn't get to sleep. She was feeling a bit queer.'

'You don't want to use that word though it's not as bad as Queersway is.'

'Don't you mean Queensway,' I said, trying hard to steady myself.

'Same thing,' he laughed.

He dropped me off. I got back inside the flat and got into bed. I couldn't fall asleep. I drummed up fantasies of girls to calm myself.

I did not ever meet Tickie again, though I did meet Charlie, who invited me to go sailing with him in the South Seas, an offer I managed to refuse. When I think back on it, I have to conclude that I was sexually ambivalent and that I was desperately seeking love, reassurance, even touch. I also sensed somehow that the great advantage of men was that they took the initiative, something that I could not do with girls even in my wildest dreams.

Miraculously I never got beaten up or into serious trouble.

I knew, of course, that if my father found out about these escapades he'd thrash the living daylights out of me. So I was worried when at our next Shabbat evening dinner, he told me he was becoming rather concerned about me.

'You mustn't go off the rails, popski,' he said.

I wondered if the porter had seen me coming in late or had seen Tickie drop me off and had decided it would be worth a bottle of whisky – or two – to report on me.

'I think, popski, that maybe someone should come to look after you.'

'I'm fine,' I protested. I hated being alone, but I was used to it.

'Shall I tell you a story about one of the Gulbenkians? You know who they are?'

I failed that bit of general knowledge and was briefed on the fact that they were immensely wealthy.

'The Gulbenkians believed that it was very important for young men not to be tempted by women of easy virtue. The young men were, of course, normal and had normal desires. When I was a young man, I had them.' He smiled. 'But what Gulbenkian did was interesting. He hired maids who were pretty and intelligent, but the maids had a secret mission.'

He had me hooked now.

'It was, of course, to teach the young men the arts of love. Cleanly. In Paris before the war there were well-regulated brothels. That is a matter of history, popski, though of course I couldn't discuss this with you if your mother were here.'

'No.'

He then changed tack. To what we would eat, to what we would drink, to the economic prospects.

'Your mother is very worried that you are too alone,' he added when we had ordered.

'I'm used to it.'

'Still, you don't want your mother to be worried.'

'I'm coping,' I said.

The following week when we had dinner he told me he had advertised for an au pair to live with me. Apparently my mother entirely approved of this scheme.

I did not particularly want to share my flat with someone I didn't know, but my father had planted the seeds with his talk of maids and secret missions. I had visions of a voluptuous au pair who would teach me the arts of love. Since she would have been told what her secret mission was, I wouldn't die of embarrassment and anxiety as I tried to work out if she would let me kiss her.

'Are you listening?' my father asked. He had finished talking about au pairs and wanted to know how well prepared I was for the O levels I would take in about three months.

'If you need extra tutors, just say. I will find the money. That is a father's duty.'

'I'm doing fine.'

'You will tell me if you have worries about the exams?' he said at the bus stop as he handed me the usual twenty pounds.

I controlled myself on the number 15 bus. I did not start daydreaming about au pairs as we passed Oxford Circus. But that night my fantasies were rich, vivid and about girls. However, my fantasies did not prepare me for Angela.

Chapter 6

Virgins and Vikings

Angela was in her early twenties. As I shook hands with her at my father's office, I could hear my mother saying, 'Well, she's no beauty'. Angela was dumpy and had a wart on her lip. She also wore – and I did not think this promising – a crucifix round her neck. My father was at his most effusive.

'So you are here to study English?' he smiled.

'Yes, I have been here three weeks,' she replied without a trace of shyness.

'And where do you come from?'

'Porto in Portugal. Where they make the port.'

'I was there before the war,' my father said. 'A lovely city. David, is there anything you want to ask?'

I had no idea what to ask but I thought I better ask something.

'Do you know about Henry the Navigator?'

Henry the Navigator was the only Portuguese person I had ever heard of. Henry the Navigator had been a big influence on navigation though he had probably never sailed far himself. But he had helped to develop the compass (which I'd forgotten to mention to Tickie) and sent ships to explore the coast of Africa circa 1450. This led to much fighting between our heroic sailors and the weevil-infested Portuguese.

'Henry the Navigator. An interesting question,' my father said.

Angela said that Henry was, of course, one of the great heroes of Portuguese history. He had helped bring Christ to the heathens.

'Mrs Cohen is where?' she then asked.

'Mrs Cohen is in Israel,' my father said.

'I did not realise that.'

'She is on family business,' my father added.

'So, in this flat you do come often, Dr Cohen?' The girl sounded like a lawyer for the prosecution.

'I have to travel for business.'

'I did not realise Mrs Cohen will not be there. But it will be okay.'

'Good,' my father said.

'I have a friend called Nina. She can stay too in the flat. My mother and father would not like me to be alone …'

She didn't finish her sentence. She didn't have to. Her very proper Portuguese mum and dad, faithful members of the Church, would not want their daughter to be alone even for a single night with a hormone-infested teenager.

My father could see that I was disappointed and broke into rapid French.

'The problem is, popski, that I have promised your mother to solve your situation,' he said.

'I can take your son to church,' Angela added to be helpful.

'We're Jewish,' I said.

'That is not problem. The Church hopes the Jews will come back to Jesus.'

Faith made Angela stubborn. She had no intention of risking herself round my hormones without protection. She could only accept the job if she could bring along her friend Nina. My father would not have to pay Nina, of course, but Nina would be around to help. 'Nina is a very nice girl,' Angela said. She had the kind of will that would have made her a Mother Superior in earlier times.

This was a total tragedy. My fantasies were dashed. I was condemned to live with two fanatically pious virgins.

'Let us see how it goes,' my father said in French.

Angela and Nina moved in the next day. Nina was dumpy like her friend. The fact that there were two of them caused an immediate problem. When I realised my father had moved out I started to sleep in my parents' double bed. Angela said it would be better if they took that room. I had no idea what to do. So I was forced to go back into my small bedroom, a bedroom I associated mainly with misery. It was from that bed that I used to implore my parents to keep quiet.

Suddenly I had no choice. I was a thirteen-year-old schoolboy who had been told he would have to live with two strangers who would contribute nothing to the great matter of making his erotic fantasies come true.

The two girls took their domestic duties seriously. They tut-tutted at the state of the flat and went on a thorough spring clean. On the first morning, they laid breakfast out on the table. Angela insisted on checking that my uniform looked clean.

She looked intently at me. I realised she was giving me the Big Sister look. Did Little Brother pass muster? She smiled and gave me a peck on the cheek.

I don't think I'd gone to school so depressed for a long time.

What I wanted of course was not a big sister.

When I got back from school, Angela and Nina were there.

'How was school?' Angela asked.

'Fine.'

She had put fruit juice and fruit and what turned out to be rather nice Portuguese cakes on the table.

'I have to work. This is where I work,' I said.

The cakes stayed where they were, and I moved all my books to the writing table in the living room.

'Henry the Navigator?' she smiled.

'Actually no. Tudors and Stuarts.'

'We watch TV to learn English.'

I was about to say that I couldn't do my homework with the television on, but in fact I often did leave it on. It was company of sorts, a human voice.

'Okay,' I said and sat down to write an essay.

At 7 p.m., Angela switched the television off and said she would now prepare dinner. Nina set the table, and a little later we sat down to eat. The food was marvellous. Angela had made a delicious fish stew which her mother had passed on to her.

But we had nothing to say to each other.

Later that evening my father rang.

'How is it going?'

'They clean and they cook rather well.'

'Good.'

I had been press-ganged into living like a spoilt but very frustrated teenager. The girls were amazingly careful to be properly dressed when I was around. First one and then the other disappeared into the bathroom to get into their night-gowns. They would reappear with dressing gowns wrapped firmly around them. They even wore slippers. I barely got a peek at an ankle.

I had got used to wandering round the flat in various states of undress – and that provoked a moral crisis. When I appeared one morning in my underpants, Angela handed me a dressing gown.

'You are nice boy,' she said. Gulbenkian would have sacked these girls after twenty-four hours.

Despite Angela's good cooking, I was being driven mad. But my father refused to take my complaints seriously. The only way I could get rid of them was to create a crisis and it suddenly became obvious to me how to go about it.

Their habits were interfering with my school work, or at least I would pretend they were. O levels were looming, and it was of 'paramount' importance to do well in them or my 'whole future will be compromised'. So I hit on a cunning plan. I deliberately started to write short and less than coherent essays.

After I had handed in two such appalling pieces of work, my master summoned me.

'Is there something wrong, Cohen?'

'No, sir.'

'Your work has been of a good standard. You're a scholar. And now you're handing in total rubbish. The damn dustman couldn't provide more rubbish,' Mr Gawne said.

'Sorry, sir.'

'Is something wrong at home?'

'Nothing's wrong, sir. Nothing's ever wrong at home, sir.'

The second phrase made him sit up. 'Nothing's ever wrong at home, sir' was too good to be true – it sounded like there *was* something going on.

'That won't do, Cohen, that won't do at all. Perhaps I should write to your parents.'

'You know best, sir.'

'Why do you suddenly sound like a robot?'

'Sorry sir,' I snapped.

'Don't be rude, boy. You'll stay in detention and I will write to your parents. I don't like your attitude at all.'

I nearly laughed. I had been living on my own for months and no one had been concerned. Turn in two bad essays – and suddenly the school took an interest.

The next day a letter for my parents arrived at Vincent Court.

I rang my father. 'There's a letter from the school for you,' I said.

'You better open it.'

'I think I'd rather bring to you.'

'I've got important meetings so I can't meet today. I'm sure it's nothing.'

The letter said that my work had taken an inexplicable nosedive. It was not worthy of a scholar and if I did work of this standard for my O levels, I would fail.

'This letter is a disgrace, David,' my father yelled. 'I'm completely ashamed of you. No teacher ever wrote a letter like that about me.'

I paused. 'It's the girls, Papa,' I said.

'I know you don't like the girls but ...'

'They watch TV all the time. I was used to doing my work in my own way and – if you want to know the truth – to wandering around the flat in my underpants ... And now I feel like I'm a prisoner.'

'You're just like your mother. A negative element.'

'Have I done badly at school before?'

'I think you have been deliberately writing bad essays to make me sack them.'

'They make it impossible for me to work.'

There was a pause. 'You haven't told your mother any of this?'

'No.'

'She is very worried about you being alone.'

'Then why doesn't she come home?' I said.

'You should ask her that. But she's never been very loyal to anyone. Apart from her bloody family.'

'Aren't we her family?'

'I think we'd better discuss this man to man,' he said suddenly. When his vitally important meeting was over, he would see me at home. I was to say nothing to Angela and Nina in the meantime.

When my father appeared at the flat, he was rather charming to them. It was not their fault, but the arrangement was not working. 'It's not that you have done anything wrong, but the sooner you can go the better.'

They were in tears. He handed them fifty pounds so they could stay in a bed and breakfast from tomorrow. He also gave them flowers and a box of chocolates. He offered to give them an excellent reference. They were completely confused.

'Don't you like us?' Angela asked after my father had left.

'I am just used to things being different.'

'You hoped we would sex with you. You're too young for sex – and I don't like boys who look fat.'

They packed their suitcases the next morning and left in a magnificent huff.

My father said we better go and have dinner together. After we had eaten at Harry Gold's he came back to the flat. He told me he would stay that night to keep an eye on me.

'The idea was good but they were the wrong kind of girls,' he said. 'But we must persevere.'

'I can't have anyone who interferes with my studying so close to O levels.'

'Of course not, popski.'

The next morning my father said that there were many vital meetings for him to attend, so we would not see each other till Friday. I have to say I heaved a sign of relief. Being alone was bad, but being with other people seemed to be worse. I moved back into the double bed.

A week later my father told me that he had had a very promising response and that I was to meet him and a possible new au pair at his office.

Monica was Finnish and blonde, and there was absolutely no sign of any religious ornament about her person.

'So you are the little boy,' she said, and she smiled a dazzling smile. As she brushed her long blonde hair back, she pushed out her boobs.

'So what do you do in the evenings?'

'Study.'

'So you're a good boy. My brother is a good boy too.' She smiled. 'I'm not a good girl.'

Please don't be, I thought but didn't say.

Monica moved in and she was what my mother would call 'a numero'. I had, and she knew I had, endless fantasies about her. That proved Tickie wrong. I wasn't queer.

Despite my raging lust I did not dare do anything. After all, I was thirteen and she was eighteen, going on thirty-five.

Monica kept the flat relatively clean but, unlike the two Portuguese girls, she was a lousy cook. She did not go in for laying out breakfast in the morning and I often ended up cooking for her. She was frequently not there because she stayed over at her boyfriend's. She knew I didn't mind and she talked about him endlessly. Charles came from the West Indies and was studying law. He had invited her to a very grand ball at the Inns of Court where she would meet judges.

Monica's other great passion was pop music, and her most precious possession was a record player. She vaguely hoped to be a dancer and she twirled for hours in the living room.

'You can dance too,' she smiled. She encouraged me to join her.

Monica didn't believe in hiding her flesh. If she had a dressing gown, I never saw it. She wore mini skirts, shorts and tops which emphasised the pouting breasts I longed to touch. If I wanted to slob around in my underpants, she couldn't have cared less.

'As long as you're ... you know ... decent,' she said in a rare moment of seriousness. She never became the wanton older woman of my dreams, but she often hugged me.

Monica knew I lusted after her so she promised that if I was a good boy and didn't tell my father she was away so much, she'd set me up with one of her friends. With Charles's help. When I finally got to meet him, I was impressed. He was a dapper West Indian with a snazzy moustache.

'You should meet some girls, David,' he said.

'I'm not interested,' I lied.

'All boys are interested in girls if they're normal, and Monica thinks you're very normal,' he smiled. 'But I remember it's not easy when you're as young as you are.'

So Monica and Charles decided to hold a party in the flat. It was to be a rather small party. Monica, Charles, me and a friend of Monica's.

I prepared for the party. I shaved. I washed my hair in the red goo I had left from the trichologist. I went out and bought some aftershave.

Monica's friend, Bettina, was a true daughter of the Vikings. She had dramatic red hair and she must have been at least eighteen. A real older woman.

We started dancing. I believed – please don't ask why after all these years – that it would impress girls if you could do Cossack dancing and I gave a passable demonstration of Cossack dancing. Everyone laughed. Then Monica changed the music to something much slower.

Charles took Monica in his arms. I looked at Bettina, unsure what to do. And then I was saved.

The flame-haired Viking took me in her arms.

We danced. She leant closer in to me, and I leant closer in to her. She moved her head back and looked me in the eyes. And then came the big moment. She leant forward and kissed me.

I had never kissed a girl before. This was the start of sex. Unfortunately my career as a kisser did not start well. I hadn't realised that you had to open your mouth and use your tongue to French kiss your partner. It didn't take me long to work that out, but I had made it quite obvious to Bettina that I was a total innocent.

Then I made a dreadful discovery. I couldn't stick my tongue out very far. I was destined to be a lousy kisser. To this day I don't know if that provoked what happened then …

The next thing I knew, Bettina bit me hard on the lip. This was another thing I hadn't realised – that kissing a girl meant she bit you till your lip bled. Bettina must have been a cannibal, or perhaps she resented the fact that her friend had set her up with a plump thirteen-year-old, or she resented the fact that I couldn't stick my tongue out very far.

But a man doesn't scream when a woman bites him, Wing Commander.

And, to be honest, I wasn't very likely to scream because, bite or no bite, I did like the way she was clinging to me.

I pressed myself, and my erection, against her. First contact. But first contact didn't become real contact. It soon became clear Bettina had no wish to bite any other part of me. So we danced and we kissed some more, and I tried to stick my tongue out further.

And then came the unexpected climax. Bettina took me by the hand and led me to the bathroom. There, in front of the mirror, she stuck her tongue out – and laughed. Her tongue protruded inches out of her mouth.

'Now you do it,' she said.

I blushed. I probably have not tried to do many things as hard as I tried to stick out my tongue. But the tip would hardly jut more than a few pathetic centimetres beyond my teeth.

'This is your problem,' Dr Bettina diagnosed.

She kissed me again and then pulled back.

'You can move your tongue side to side,' she smiled. And she ruffled my hair. I obviously wasn't destined to be her great passion.

At midnight Monica said she was going off to stay with Charlie.

Why don't you stay Bettina, I thought but I had no idea of how to say it.

'I have to go too,' she said quickly. 'I had a nice time.' She gave me a last playful hug and a quick kiss. 'Remember, side to side,' she laughed – and went off with Monica and Charlie.

The flat seemed very quiet again. I piled up the glasses and dirty dishes in the kitchen and went to bed. As I did so, I was acutely aware that I needed a team of medical experts before I even managed to pet with someone. The hair doctor was required to stop me going bald, I couldn't shut my left eye without shutting both eyes, and now I probably needed a tongue specialist.

I lusted after Monica and Bettina, but I knew perfectly well that I was not in love with either of them. The reason was simple. I had a huge crush on a woman I knew quite well, my cousin Rita.

Rita worked as an assistant for the famous film producer Otto Preminger. She was married to an architect called Lulu who considered himself to be one of the most gifted architects of his generation. They lived in Paris in a very smart apartment. Rita was blonde and willowy. She must have been in her thirties. She had an Afghan hound she adored.

Twice during this period, she invited me to stay with her and her husband in Paris. Nothing was ever said about the situation in London. When I stayed with them, the Afghan hound often lay on my feet. I didn't protest because I was so devoted to Rita.

Rumour – i.e. my mother's strudel-eating friends – had it that Rita had had an affair with Paul Newman during the filming of *Exodus*, which was directed by Preminger. I didn't dare ask her about that. The best evidence for this rumoured affair was that Lulu had left Rita, according to the strudel eaters at least.

'But Lulu he's a film star and you are massively fat,' Rita had said to her husband – or so I was told.

'But is he a brilliant architect?' Lulu replied.

To which there was no answer. My dreams of Rita were run-of-the-mill erotic, but I knew perfectly well that this was a love I had to keep secret. I could hardly hope to compete with Paul Newman and one of the great – if very fat – architects of our time.

Rita gave me a book called *The Art of Dating* because she

realised I was getting to that age. It revealed that teenagers had feelings. It explained how the wondrous world of love lay ahead of us. It explained how to kiss a girl and also how to behave if the girl didn't want to be kissed. Though it was heterosexual, it was certainly not about getting your end away. Boy meets girl. Boy kisses girl. Boy wants to touch girl. But woe betide boy who can not keep a grip on his hormones. The book did not advise on tongue gymnastics or tell you how you should behave if your date bit you and drew blood. *The Art of Dating* was the product of an innocent world.

Meanwhile, in London, Monica hoped that Charles was going to pop the question at the judge-filled ball. He didn't. She became depressed and went back to Finland but promised she would be back after the holidays.

Again, more must have been going on than I realised because, among my father's papers, I found copies of letters Monica had written to my mother. She told her that 'David is doing well at school and is a very nice boy. We went to the theatre with Dr Cohen last Friday.'

I was a few months off being fourteen and scared I was going to stay innocent for far too long. Every time I looked in the mirror, I was sure no girl would look twice at me. Bettina, I now decided, had kissed me as a favour to Monica – and anyway she had this bad habit of biting. All the mirror told me was that I was losing my hair and I had pimples all over my face. The pimples made me desperate. I tried to shave them off and only succeeded in making my face bleed.

Somehow through all this chaos, I managed to get my nine O levels – and nearly all of them with good grades. My father insisted on a slap-up dinner at the Ecu de France.

I seized the moment to ask if I could go to Israel.

'I shall borrow the money from the bloody bank manager,' my father smiled. Nothing pleased him more than when I passed exams. 'You deserve a reward for having done so well.'

Because of my father's habit of keeping the papers, I still have the report I got from St Paul's. It was pretty good and said I was quite mature for a boy of my age.

If only they knew why.

As my father walked me back to the bus stop, I felt suddenly very close to him.

'Now, with results like that, popski, I'm sure you can go to Oxbridge,' he beamed. And gave me an extra fiver.

I knew better than to tell him what I would really be doing in the next few weeks. I had a big project in mind. If it worked out, I wouldn't be going to his fabled Oxbridge.

It remained one of my two secret ambitions to become an actor and a playwright. As soon as I finished sitting my O levels, I bought a notebook with a dark-blue cover and committed myself to the play I had been thinking about. I poured my heart into *The Flood*.

My play was the tragic story of a twelve-year-old boy. Unlike me, the hero lived on Pineapple Island, which was somewhere in the South Atlantic. Not so unlike me, the boy has been abandoned and betrayed, and he takes his revenge on the world. It opened with an unusual plea to the audience.

The Child: Please don't listen. I'm not supposed to speak, I do a lot of things I'm not supposed to do.

I have always kept the manuscript of *The Flood*. With it, I found a way of expressing my distress. I have already mentioned the 'cry for help'. *The Flood* was a cry for help and then some. Because it is so raw, it is worth reproducing some of it.

The only people who lived on the island were the owner of the pineapple plantation, his butler, his son, his gardener, a fundamentalist priest, who was always trying to collect money for his church, and the son's girlfriend. When the priest is not trying to scrounge money, he is working on his magnum opus – *The Pineapple*, a study of its history and exotic recipes. In fact, it's not quite true that no one else lived on the island. There were also a thousand pineapple workers but they stayed well off-stage. For no reason I can explain, an immensely rich American couple, Mr and Mrs Bockenheimer, turn up on the island. (This is quite a feat as the island is off all known shipping lanes and does not have an airport.) They are accompanied by their butler, who has been employed to write Mrs Bockenheimer's memoirs. 'Mrs Bockenheimer is worth her weight in gold though of course only the Bank of England keeps that much gold,' the butler says.

At the end of Act One, the gardener announces that the sea level is rising and that within days they will all drown. No one will come to their rescue because the island is so remote and the only radio set is dead because the gardener forgot to order new batteries. 'The *News of the World* will say Island Disappears.' The father is accused of being a bully and an exploiter, but what I find interesting is that there is no mother. There is no explanation for her absence, it is simply a matter of fact, a fact that, of course, reflected the reality of my life.

The child watches all the action and only speaks at the start and end of the play. The son of the owner – none of the characters had names – surveys the wreck as all the islanders have drowned, jumped off the nearest cliff, shot themselves in the head or been bitten by snakes. I had it in for humanity, it seems.

Son of the owner: So now they've all gone except the Child. I wish you could talk.

The Child: I can.

Son: Can you? You must have laughed at us, we deserve to be laughed at.

Child: Yes.

Son: You enjoyed it, didn't you, seeing eight humans make a mockery of humanity? All useless persons apart from the priest and the gardener and the American. He had a handful with his wife.

Child: Silly woman. Tipped well though.

Son: It's funny but we never gave you the right to speak. You have it though from birth like everyone else. They forgot all about you, didn't they? Your very existence was forgotten. I forgot about you too till now.

There follows a lot of apocalyptic stuff in which the son denounces his father and warns that while the island 'will crumble into the sea', the child will somehow survive. The cunning child then asks if he can have the 'deeds of the island' so that no one can dispute his ownership and points out that he has given the son a lock of a girl's hair. Then the son hands over the island and a mysterious girl, Peg, to the child, who is literally going to inherit the earth, or the island at least. If only the flood waters recede. It all ends with the child, as predicted, somehow surviving.

I had no idea what to do with this play when I finished it. Then I saw an advertisement which said that a new theatre was opening in Croydon. The Ashcroft Theatre offered a prize of a hundred guineas for the best play. I got to work on the Olivetti I used to forge absentee notes. When I had finished, I added at the end of my typescript that I had completed *The Flood* two days after my fourteenth birthday 'when I was feeling desperately alone, as I have for the last 3 years'. (I didn't dare say I was living alone, but I did want to twang the violins.)

It worked. One day a letter arrived at Vincent Court. It announced that the judges had decided to award me a special prize of ten guineas. I was invited to the presentation at the theatre.

Peggy Ashcroft, the great actress, was going to present the prizes and other important people would be there. The *Daily Telegraph* reported the fact that a St Paul's schoolboy had won a prize. Given all the fuss, I was amazed – and hurt – that my mother didn't come back from Israel. She adored the theatre. I was even more amazed by my father. He loved the theatre and knew a lot about it. He was apparently too busy to come. Instead, he sent one of his secretaries, a Mrs Walker (who must have replaced Mrs Brown), to accompany me. The distance from Norbury where he lived to Croydon is 3 miles.

At the presentation, no one seemed surprised that a fourteen-year-old boy should turn up without his parents.

Mrs Walker wrote my father a memo about how I behaved. It took me years to realise that my parents must have been envious as well as totally self-absorbed. This was real worldly success. My father, I realise now, couldn't cope with it. When I published my first book fifteen years later, I sent him a copy. He did not speak to me for a year! He had been such a bright boy in pre-war Palestine, he had got all those degrees – but he had never even published a memo.

Mrs Walker's memo told my father that she had been very pleased to see me presented with the prize of ten guineas. Peggy Ashcroft had asked if there were any questions but no one had any. There was a BBC film unit and Peggy Ashcroft was interviewed – and so was I for half a minute. I had made the news! Mrs Walker told the reporters that she was there on my father's behalf, but she was not invited to come to lunch with the prizewinners. I don't remember anything about the lunch, but my early success convinced me that I had made the right career choice. The theatre was my future.

I even got letters from agents who wanted to meet me. I might be a promising young man they could represent. One was called Mary Leigh and she would have a surprising influence on my life.

Suddenly everything seemed to be going right. I auditioned for a part in the new school play, Marlowe's *Dr Faustus*. To my delight I got the lead. I was overjoyed. The bright lights of the West End shone in my eyes. I might have problems with my mother, my father and girls, but I was going to play the lead.

And boys who wrote plays and played the lead must surely get the girls ...

Chapter 7

Secret Lovers

For once my father was as good as his word. A few days after we had celebrated my O-level triumph, he told me he had booked me on a flight to Athens. Again I realised that my parents had communicated about me without my knowing. My mother would meet me there because he had asked her to visit an old associate of his, a Greek shipping magnate called Xydias. Xydias might lend him money, I presumed.

'Xydias tells me that he is always being nagged by women to marry him,' my father explained. 'And he says, "Why should I make one woman unhappy when I can make many happy?"'

My mother came to meet me at the airport. But she wasn't alone. She was talking to a handsome woman called Tula, who, I discovered, was Xydias's mistress. My mother said she was proud of me for having done so well in my exams.

'It can't have been too terrible not to have me there,' she smiled.

'I ...'

'Your father tells me you had some interesting experiences with au pairs.'

'That's not true.' I couldn't be rude in front of Tula.

'Au pairs are nearly as bad as secretaries,' she pronounced.

Tula's flat was on Lykabettos, the huge hill from where you look down on the Acropolis. She had a great sense of design and everything inside was supremely elegant. I was put in the maid's room as the maid had gone to stay with her family while we visited.

My mother came into my room and asked how my father was, and if he had sent any letters.

'No.'

'Good. He never has anything pleasant to say.'

She gave me a quick kiss and went back to talk with her friend. Tula still hoped that Xydias would marry her.

When my mother walked out of the room I didn't feel desperate as I had in Israel, not desperate to talk to her, not desperate to get her to stay longer.

The next day my mother and Tula had planned a morning of culture followed by an afternoon of shopping. After walking up the Acropolis, I had to follow them into Athens's smartest shops. My mother was obviously not short of money.

'My brother Relly has given me some money,' she said by way of explanation.

This was about as likely as the Pope becoming a Buddhist, but I just shrugged.

Tula had a younger sister, Leila, who must have been in her twenties. That evening she said we must all go to a nightclub. Leila was funny, lanky and lively. She inspected me while my mother was getting dressed,

'Don't you have a tie?' Leila said.

'No.'

'You'll need a tie. I'll get one of Xydias's.'

She rummaged in a cupboard, found one and started to tie it around my neck.

'This is a nice thing a girl can do for a boy but don't get any ideas. I have a fiancé and how old are you?'

'Nearly fifteen,' I exaggerated.

'So young. You should be in school.'

'I am in school.'

Leila drove us to the club, which was near the Athens race course. It was one of the swankiest places I have ever been to and I suspect you did not get in unless a multimillionaire introduced you. Mr Xydias kissed Tula, kissed Leila and kissed my mother. He was small and fat but he exuded authority. He was very polite to my mother, asked about my father and told us to order whatever we liked. He then disappeared to talk business with some other mogul.

A little later, Xydias returned. 'I want to introduce you to some friends,' he smiled.

We followed him to a large table where a large man and a dark dramatic woman were sitting. They were his friends Aristotle Onassis and the great singer Maria Callas, whom Onassis eventually left for Jackie Kennedy.

They smiled at us. Leila realised we weren't remotely interesting to them, smiled sweetly and said, 'I am going to take my young friend dancing.'

Leila danced like a whirlwind. Monica had also danced fast and I'd learned to keep up with her. Leila nodded, 'You dance fast but you're still too young for me.'

'And you have a fiancé.'

'I was lying about that but you're still too young for me.'

I was too plain, too intense, too young, too plump, always not quite right … When was I going to meet a girl who thought I was adequate enough to let me get in her knickers?

It was certainly not going to happen in Athens. Leila took me out one afternoon and I was glad to go because there was a sense of real strain between me and my mother. She did not want to discuss when she was coming back to London. She did not want to discuss why the flat on Mount Carmel had still not been sold.

Then, my mother told me there was a change of plan. We wouldn't be going on to Israel but to Switzerland.

'Don't you have to be there to sell the flat?' I said.

The estate agent was showing it to many people, all the time, day and night, she assured me. It was important that we went to Switzerland.

As we took off for Geneva, my mother said that we would probably meet Mr Soussi and that she wanted me to be nice to him.

'I'm always polite,' I said sceptically.

She pressed my hand and said, 'Mon petit. Please don't tell your father.'

So I discovered that Soussi was 'probably a suitor', as my mother put it coyly. She could not help it if she had swept him off his feet. Women did that, and she still had her looks, though she had no idea for how much longer. As we landed, she turned intently to me.

'I know you love me and I know you love your father,' she said, 'but you know what your father is like. A fou furieux.' As she said it, it dawned on me that I had not seen my father in a rage for well over a year now. He had not tried to hit me for ages.

But for her he remained the man who was always liable to fly into a rage – and who was often unjust. Casanova Cohen had once discovered that she had had dinner with a certain Mr Berkowitz, 'who was a friend of the family, David, nothing more'. My father didn't just lose his temper with her, but made a disgraceful scene in a smart restaurant in Paris, threatening to beat Berkowitz 'black and blue' if he ever tried to seduce his wife again. She relied on me to be a good son to her, which meant, of course, keeping quiet about Soussi.

Soussi was at the airport to meet her, no 'probably' about it. He kissed her but on the cheek. He tried to kiss me on the cheek but I insisted on just shaking his hand. My mother, it seemed to me, was always ambivalent about him. She enjoyed the fact that he was besotted with her and yet she couldn't help being slightly mocking about him. I hope I'll be forgiven if I am less than fair in my description of my mother's suitor.

As I have mentioned, Soussi was fat and past the help even of my trichologist. He looked, in fact, a little like the actor in the famous ad for Hamlet cigars who desperately combs his few strands of remaining hair over his pink pate. His wife had died around the time in 1956 when Soussi had left Egypt, taking his money with him, so that he was both available and – and this mattered to my mother – rich. My mother kindly agreed to teach Soussi the art of shopping.

I may sound cynical as I write this now, but I believed in my mother's innocence completely. I never dreamed anything physical could be going on between her and this grandfatherly figure who looked like a pear-shaped balloon.

I suspect I oozed hostility, but Soussi still tried to make friends with me. But there was a problem, in fact two problems. First, I regarded him as a monster and had no intention of being anything other than icily polite. The second problem was Soussi's ginger-haired son, Dennis, who was more or less my age.

In my mind I called him Dennis the Menace. Dennis was fiercely loyal to the memory of his mother, who had died not long ago. He was hostile to my mother, who was taking his father away. Now it seems totally normal, but at the time I hated the fact that he was as rude to my mother as I was to his father.

It wouldn't have mattered but we were often left to our own devices during this holiday. In the middle of the summer in the Swiss mountains, there is nothing for angry teenagers to do. My mother controlled Soussi totally, and he was obliged to go shopping for most of the day and for the rest of it to visit museums. Art would be good for the Soussi soul, which lacked depth. Because of the unfortunate fact that he had lived in Egypt, and the less unfortunate fact he had been busy making a fortune, the Soussi soul was in dire need of stimulation and development.

'I am so good for that man,' my mother said in one of the few moments when we were alone together. 'I hope that you and Dennis are getting on.'

What do two hostile teenagers forced together do? We played angry games of table tennis which Dennis tended to win. We never spoke much. I think he was even more furious at the situation than I was. He converted that energy more effectively into aggressive forehands and backhands.

I wished we were back in Cannes, where we could go swimming or I could walk up the mountains to Le Cannet. When I asked my mother, she said that she did not want to introduce Soussi to Laura and Zoli, who also usually took holidays in Cannes. I think she was ashamed of him really.

After two weeks in Athens and Switzerland, my mother said that she had to return to Israel. She had talked to my father and I was to return to London.

I minded, but I didn't mind that much. Anything to escape from Soussi and Dennis.

My mother took me to Geneva airport by herself for once.

'I know this is hard for you,' she said, 'but I'm very proud of you. Life isn't easy,' she added, 'your father doesn't make life easy.' But she wouldn't explain any more.

When I got back to London, my father questioned me. Where had I gone with my mother? Who else was there? And there was also the continuing sore point. Did I have any idea why she had not sold the flat?

'She could have sold the Taj Mahal and the Tower of Babel more rapidly. But of course she does not want to sell the flat because she refuses to realise the seriousness of the situation.'

I said nothing.

'That fake Communist Berg is still threatening to bankrupt me,' my father complained. 'If your mother did what she promised to do, Berg would be neutralised.'

But I was completely loyal to my mother and never told my father a word about Soussi.

So I went back to living alone in Vincent Court and started to prepare for my A levels. There were no more au pairs – the heartbroken Monica did not return – but my father arranged for a cleaner to come once a week. We resumed our routine of meeting on Friday nights. He told me that in view of my good results he had decided to up my housekeeping money by two pounds a week.

I wrote less and less to my mother.

If you live on your own you have plenty of time and freedom to search every nook and cranny of your home. Both my parents kept papers and they intrigued me.

Soon after I got back, I went on a rummage. There was not much storage space in the flat but there was a small cellar in the basement of the block where we were allowed to leave stuff. My parents had left two boxes in there – marked 'White Knight Laundry'.

One day not long after returning, I brought one of these boxes back upstairs and started to go through its contents. One folder was marked 'Private and Confidential'. It wasn't very thick. I took it out and stared at it. I knew perfectly well that I shouldn't open it. After a few minutes, I did exactly that.

Inside there were a number of documents in Hebrew and some in Romanian. And then I found a marriage certificate from Bucharest in 1938. It recorded the marriage at the British Embassy of Benjamin Cohen LLD and a certain Mrs Dolly Kertesz. I didn't understand. My mother's maiden name was Cappon. Who in the name of heaven was this Mrs Kertesz?

The obvious person to ask was my father, who must surely know who he had married. But how could I explain the question without admitting that I had opened up the folder marked 'Private'. The heroes in the *Boy's Own* adventures never had to face a problem like this.

I decided to wait until the next Friday when I went to his office.

'The porter told me he had to bring up some of our boxes because they were taking up too much room,' I lied.

My father was rarely bothered about such practical matters.

'He was careless – probably had too much whisky – and some papers fell out,' I said. 'One was your marriage certificate.' And then I added, 'I expect it was something to do with giving the Nazis the slip.'

He looked blankly at me.

'Who gave the Nazis the slip?'

'Mama.'

'The only time your mother's family met any Nazis was to give them bribes,' my father sniped.

It was time to ask the all-important question.

'I don't understand why the marriage certificate was not in her maiden name of Cappon. I thought it must be to do with escaping the Nazis?'

'You really shouldn't look in people's private papers,' he said. But he wasn't furious as I had expected him to be. In fact he was laughing. 'Your mother always pretends that I am the one with secrets. But when I met her she had a secret of her own. I'll tell you when we have dinner,' he added.

I was so relieved that he hadn't gone berserk that I was quite prepared to wait. He collected his coat and his hat and we walked down into Jermyn Street and to the Ecu de France.

After he had ordered wine and poured me some – 'to steady your nerves, popski' – my father started laughing.

'When I went to Bucharest to meet your mother's family, I wasn't looking for a wife at all. But they pushed her at me and, then, I discovered that she had been married. But the marriage had gone wrong.'

'Gone wrong in what way?'

'Just gone wrong. She made me promise not to tell you anything about this catastrophe. And, of course, it was a catastrophe.'

'Then why are you laughing?'

He looked down at his plate, suppressed his laughter and poured us more wine.

'Shabbat shalom, *mon petit*,' he said. 'You must promise not to ask your mother about it.'

'Why?'

'Because I am asking you to.'

'But was she married before?'

'Yes.'

'And who was Kertesz?'

'A man who worked with her father.'

'And what happened?'

'My lips are sealed. And if you are a gentleman, you will never raise the subject with your mother. Now tell me about school.'

So my mother had had a husband before my father, and she was now allowing Soussi the status of a suitor. I was not supposed to know about Kertesz and I was not supposed to talk about Soussi.

In some way that I never understood, my parents still communicated with each other. Though my father had told me that his lips were sealed, a few days later I got a letter from my mother. She said that she knew that I had been going through her papers, which was a dirty thing to do because papers were sacred and private. She hoped I had not said anything worrying about our holiday to my father.

She wrote in French and her phrase was '*des choses qui pourraient nous faire des soucis*'. *Soucis* means 'worries'. You didn't have to be a code-breaker to realise that she was talking about Soussi and asking me not to say we had been in Switzerland with him.

Then she added that, at the time of the event to which the papers referred, she had been very young. She and Mr Kertesz both liked to ride motorbikes and they had decided, as friends, that they would ride their motor bikes across part of the Sahara. In those days it was not possible for a man and a woman to go motorbiking together in Arab countries without being married.

So in order to get visas – and even petrol – she had had to get married to this Mr Kertesz. Of course, Mr Kertesz was a gentleman and nothing happened. And when my father turned up, he at once gave her a divorce.

I knew quite well that this was a lie. I couldn't help wondering just what had gone wrong in my mother's first marriage. I was hurt that she refused to tell me. Between ex-husbands and secret suitors, I was beginning to wonder who my mother really was.

I would eventually find out the truth about Kertesz, but my mother's first marriage was not the worst of the secrets I had still to uncover.

Chapter 8
Pretending

I sometimes wonder whether happy teenagers have less insistent hormones, a subject psychology hasn't studied as far as I can tell. Winning the playwriting prize gave me something else I'd never expected – a real triumph with which to try and impress girls. And somehow the courage to go to clubs like the Witches in Hampstead and the Macabre, where every table was shaped liked a coffin. In the 1960s it was quite usual for a fourteen-year-old to go to clubs.

In the gloom of the Witches, I saw two pretty girls. The problem was always how to break the ice. Some equally hormoned lad had shown me the 'matchbox trick'. You asked a girl for a match, lit your cigarette and then gave her back not the matchbox, but the dead match.

'Very clever,' said the dark angular girl. 'We'll talk to you anyway.'

Judith and her glamorous blonde friend, Anne, were both a lot older. Both were as English as roses and they were looking for something exotic you didn't find in Slough or St Albans, where they came from.

Judith had lost her mother and was as needy as I was. Finally here was the older woman – she was all of twenty-two – who was going to put me out of my virginal misery. And I'd found her all by myself. I didn't, of course, tell Judith I'd never done it before.

Judith shared a flat with Anne on Haverstock Hill, which leads up from Chalk Farm to Hampstead Village. I can't now remember how many dates we had, but it was not many before she took me back there. I'd been dreaming of this moment for the last three or four years. Judith was very sweet. She guessed, of course, that I was a virgin, took me by the hand and led me inside. Now, thinking back on it, I think that what I felt most of all was totally grateful. I'm sure that on that first night I was not much of a lover. I don't remember anything specific about the night but so odd is the memory that I still remember the address – 166B Haverstock Hill.

Once it was clear that Judith and I were lovers, I got to meet Anne's boyfriend. She had hit the jackpot in the matter of exotic love. Roy Sawh came from British Guiana and spoke at Speaker's Corner. He was a Communist like Red Berg and just as eccentric. He'd won a scholarship to Moscow University but had been deported from the Soviet Union within weeks. He'd tried to set up a Black Student Group there and the KGB was having none of that.

'I've never seen such racism,' Roy laughed. And as I got to know him, I realised there was plenty in England. He was nice to me, though he could be sharp with his words when the need arose. Once a woman at Speaker's Corner heckled him.

'You're not like us,' she screamed, 'you're a bloody monkey. Go back to the jungle.'

Roy made himself as tall as he could on his platform. 'You are right madam, I am not like you,' he said. 'I am a British subject. You are a British object.'

Everyone laughed.

Roy was a showman and extremely confident with women. He had no idea where this confidence came from but he exuded it and I envied him. He was not especially good-looking but that didn't matter. Anne was utterly besotted.

As I say, I was needy and Judith was needy. I had a flat. We were having a good time. We didn't agonise or discuss our relationship. Within weeks, she brought her two suitcases – only two, Judith wasn't all that interested in clothes – round to Vincent Court. She also brought a few pots and pans. So suddenly I was living with a woman. What would the High Master say …

Is this true, Cohen? Living with a woman?

Yes, sir.

In the biblical sense?

Well, sir, the Israelites were up to it all the time.

I was not as well versed in the Bible as I am now, having since spent eighteen months producing films about it. If I had been, I could have rattled off not merely the long lists of who begat whom but, of course, the best saucy sections – the Song of Solomon, the antics of King David and the bizarre episode where Lot's daughters lie with him because he is the only man around. It's surprising no one has made a film called *The Bible's Naughty Bits*.

Living with Judith was fun.

Anna and Roy also often stayed the night in the flat. I was very amused when, one night, I saw Roy in his long johns. My father also wore long johns and I had once seen him go completely berserk – about the fall in oil shares – in them.

This was one of the less likely legacies of the British Empire
– colonials from hot countries loved long johns.

I was very happy until one day when I got home early
from school to discover Judith sitting on someone else's lap.
I just turned and left. I walked the streets around Seymour
Place as I had when I couldn't wait any longer for my mother
to return to the flat.

I rang before I went back. Judith answered and said she
was going out. She didn't know when she'd be back.

I was once more waiting for a woman to return, but I
was older now – and knew how to cope. I got drunk.
Late in the evening Judith returned and that night she
made love more passionately to me than ever before. So
I forgave her even though part of me wished I'd been
brave enough to say that that was it. Being left hurts your
self-esteem, but I have never found it easy to end relationships. Even when my head tells me that it would be
the best thing to do.

So Judith and I stayed together. My father liked her.
More than thirty years and two psychology degrees later,
I can explain why I sometimes act the way I do. There is
no gene that makes you passive-aggressive, I think. The
concept was developed by, among others, the American
psychiatrist Aaron Beck, who is famous for his Depression
Scale. Passive-aggressive personalities see themselves as
self-sufficient but feel that others misunderstand and
want to control them. They become dependent, but
dislike that dependency so much that they protest against
it – sometimes by appeasing too much, sometimes by
being too aggressive and, sometimes, by being just plain
devious.

You are devious because you are angry and you see
yourself as a victim, but you lack a certain bedrock of

confidence and so you avoid confrontation. But you don't give up or give in. Caught in the middle of these competing impulses, you get your own back sneakily.

It's something I have often been accused of doing. And I have to admit, by the time I was sixteen, I had became skilled at it – too skilled for my own good.

I never consciously decided to get my own back on Judith, but it happened and I'm sure I meant it to happen. I met a girl called Olivia at some acting classes I was taking. Olivia was a willowy blonde. She had an almost perfectly oval face. She lived in Chelsea with her parents, who were something in the arts. She was studying art herself.

Olivia was sixteen and, I realise now, she was either scared of sex or didn't fancy me enough. Every time we got close to making love she would tense up. I had, I suspect, all the sexual subtlety of an overexcited gorilla, and so I had no idea how to make her feel relaxed or that sex could be fun. Still, I continued to go out with her, and more times than I care to remember I had to practise the Zen art of persuading my erection to go away. At some point I became stubborn and decided I was going to make love to Olivia.

By now it was the summer again, and one day I was reading *The Times* and saw a cottage in France advertised. (I was not going to spend another summer with my mother and Mr Soussi and Dennis.) I was doing well at school, and I thought my father could be persuaded to cough up the money needed to rent it. I was right and I asked Olivia if she wanted to come too. She was only sixteen, like me, but her parents were arty-liberal. To my amazement, she agreed.

My problem now was Judith. I could hardly tell her I was

going on holiday with another girl or, at least, that's what I felt. So she was absolutely not to do what it would have been perfectly natural for her to do – come to Victoria Station to see me off.

I racked my brains. My only hope, I decided, was to go into mystic mode. A few days before my departure, I told Judith I'd had terrible nightmares, premonitions, things that went bump in the mind. These most dreadful portents – I knew my Shakespeare, and Shakespeare provides plenty of stories to compare your worst dreams against – meant that I didn't want anyone to see me off.

Not even her.

I'm pretty sure I was convincing because I really was scared of what would happen if Judith did come to Victoria and saw me with Olivia. And fear worked.

It is possible, of course, that Judith saw through my whole charade and couldn't be bothered to turn it into a great scene. Or maybe she had reasons of her own for not doing so. But as far as I was concerned, I had pulled it off. I'm not proud of it now, but I had learned that deception wasn't just for school.

So Olivia and I left for Bauduen, a tiny village in Provence where we stayed in a small flat, swam in the river, got friendly with the local priest and marvelled at the town hall whose shelves had land deeds going back to 1578. Olivia and I did finally make love. The priest knew what was going on perfectly well – he had retired to Bauduen from Cannes. He could no longer bear to hear the confessions of film stars, he told us, something that impressed us greatly.

Having intervened for the souls of great cinematic sinners, he didn't think our sin worth bothering about – and, of course, I was a Jew and Olivia wasn't a Catholic.

In France, Olivia and I had a better time than I had

expected, but there was no real chemistry between us. I wasn't too worried about that. My cocky teenage self was certain that as soon as I got back to England, my life was going to change dramatically.

And 'dramatically' was the word.

Chapter 9

Minehead and Oxford

In all of this, my bravest decision was to quit school the moment I had done my A levels. Both of my parents had drummed into me the value of education. My father wanted me to be a lawyer. My A-level results were very good and in those days the masters of St Paul's spoke to their friends in Oxbridge colleges. I was told I had a guaranteed place at Oxford – and at Christ Church – and it was considered an outrage that I didn't want to take it up.

But I had got the stage bug. It had started back at Eaton House, where I had been cast – because I was fat – as Falstaff in a cut-down version of *The Merry Wives of Windsor*. The play was directed by our English teacher, Mr Buckland. I suspect my performance was not subtle. I loved belching on stage, which Falstaff has to do. I managed to tumble into the laundry basket in which Falstaff is carried out of the house when the husband of one of the merry wives he has been chatting up appears. Every laugh I got made me feel wonderful.

(The part of Mrs Page was taken by Alan Yentob, who was also at the school. He went on to a glittering career at the BBC.)

In my first year at St Paul's, I joined the drama society. The school play was, as I have mentioned, Moliere's *The Miser*. I obviously was not a useless actor, though I was too new in my first year to get a proper part. Instead I understudied the lead, played by David Aukin, who went on to his own glittering career in British television. In my second year I got my reward. After a tense series of auditions, I was told that the director had decided that I would be better as Faustus than as Mephistopheles.

I still have my copy of the play and I can still recite the opening lines: 'Settle thy studies, Faustus, and begin / to sound the depth of that thou wilt profess'.

In the opening scene, Faustus dismisses theology, philosophy, medicine and law, 'a petty case of paltry legacies'. The one study that is worth pursuing is magic. The necromancer can control the world and so Faustus sells his soul to the Devil, or at least to the Devil's representative, Mephistopheles. The contract has to be signed in blood. For twenty-four years Faustus has tremendous fun, but then he has to pay the price. I can still feel the thrill of doing the last lines when Faustus begs for repentance but it is too late and the jaws of hell open to greet him.

People were very flattering about my Dr Faustus. (I should note that I had lost a good deal of weight since playing Falstaff.) It went to my head. I was going to be a great actor and I was not going to bother with anything so banal as going to Oxford. I had managed to cope all on my own thus far.

After *Dr Faustus*, I bought a copy of *The Stage* and wrote to any number of agents. Most didn't answer, but Mary

Leigh, who had written to me after I had won the prize in the playwriting competition, invited me to come and see her. She and her husband, Charles Guy, ran an agency in Sackville Street in Mayfair. She was the kind of theatrical character you really don't see any more. Her face was caked with make-up. Charles Guy was very small and very nervous, and Mrs Leigh, as we all had to call her, spoke with a fake cut-glass accent.

I was shaking, of course.

'You better show me what you can do, dear. You do have an audition speech ...'

I'm sure I did something from *Richard III*.

'Ah, dear Shakespeare. We don't do Shakespeare in Minehead.'

I desperately wanted to know what she thought of my performance.

'Obviously you can't act professionally yet, but I could take you on as an Assistant Stage Manager.'

I was ecstatic.

'And you could understudy and play small parts.'

'Wonderful.'

Of course, there could be no question of my being paid. I was not a member of Equity, the actors' and stage managers' union. I was still just under sixteen. But I was obviously intelligent. I had to realise that being an ASM involved sweeping the stage and making tea and coffee for the 'mature artistes'.

When I told my father that I would not be going to Oxford, I could see that he wanted to hit me. But he managed to restrain himself and just shouted.

'Have you any idea what you're doing?'

My father yelled that I was insane and ungrateful. I could never be on the board of ICI if I didn't go to Oxbridge. And he had slaved for all these years to pay the exorbitant school fees just so that I could go to Oxbridge.

'Do you think these English bastards will forgive you if you make music in their faces?'

As I mentioned, 'making music' was his way of saying 'fart'.

He told me to go away and think again.

But the more I thought about it, the surer I was. My mother rang to say I had upset my father terribly. And her. She followed it up with letters begging me not to be reckless. It was true that some actors were magnificent – and she had named me Oliver after Laurence Olivier – but it was a wretched life for most of them. They never knew where their next penny was coming from. Did I want to live like that? She was a rich girl who would be haunted all her life by the fear of poverty.

Then the High Master of St Paul's summoned me to say he was dreadfully disappointed by my irrational decision. It would be very difficult for him to give me a decent reference if I were to show such a lack of consideration for the teachers who had guided me so devotedly. I had already upset T. E. B. Howarth, who had replaced the Reverend Gilkes as High Master, by writing a critical article about the school in the school magazine.

I began to waver in the face of all this pressure. But then my father rang me to say that he wanted to see me in his office at once.

I walked, shaking, up the stairs at 57 Jermyn Street. I kept on saying to myself that I wanted to do this and that I would be one of the great actors of my time.

He was alone.

'I have been giving serious consideration to your request.'

I hadn't requested anything, I thought.

'A young man has to have his fun, his folly. Some boys go to sea. And this place Minehead is by the coast.'

'Yes.'

'I insist, of course, on meeting this Mary Leigh person before giving my final decision. But I'm inclined to think you'd better get it out of your system, popski,' he said. 'How much is this woman paying you?'

'Two pounds,' I lied.

'And how were you going to eat?' Sometimes my father could go out of his way to humiliate people but on that important day he did not humiliate me. 'You calculated that your father would not let you starve. And if you turn out to be a great actor, good.'

The meeting between my father and Mary Leigh was a coming together of two great egos, neither of whom had done what they had hoped to in life – he had expected to be a great advocate, she a great actress. My father found out in due course that I had lied about the two pounds but said that he would 'defray all expenses'. He also urged Mrs Leigh to put on at least one Shakespeare play in order to raise the tone in Minehead.

'My dear Dr Cohen, sadly the public in Minehead is not ready for Shakespeare,' she said.

So at the age of fifteen years and nine months, former Cadet and St Paul's Scholar Cohen took the train down to the sleepy Somerset town of Minehead. I had not arranged anywhere to stay. The leading man, who was named John, said that it was a bit late now to find digs, but I could come and stay with him. Once at his place, he knocked back a few whiskies, offered me some and when I asked where the spare bed was, shook his head.

'You sleep that side,' he smiled.

After Tickie it should it have occurred to me that John

had not invited me back to his digs without an ulterior motive. But – for once – sex was the last thing on my mind. I was so excited to be in a real theatre company.

A few minutes later I felt John's hand creep on to my shoulder and start to rub it. But now there was no temptation.

'I'm not like that, I've had girlfriends,' I said, and I took his hand off my shoulder.

'I'll be very gentle,' he said.

I'd heard those words before. I sat bolt upright and said that if he didn't mind I'd sleep in his armchair. He didn't protest. At about five in the morning, I got dressed and walked into the town. I managed to find myself some digs before I had to report at the theatre at 10 a.m.

I was terrified that John would refer to this incident, and hold it against me, but he never did. He was a gentle and sad man who presided over the unlikely-ever-to-succeed players of weekly rep in Minehead. I made tea, handled the prompt book and was in thespian heaven.

I hadn't been there long when I was told that I had been cast in next week's play. I rang my father and he said that of course he would be there for the first night. This was really bizarre. I had won a prize in a national competition and he couldn't come three miles, but he could travel the 150 miles to Minehead. I didn't understand then. Today, I suspect the answer is simple. For your son to act in a tacky rep is nothing to be envious of. It is somewhat different for your son to win a prize in a national competition.

But then something extraordinary happened. The lady at the box office appeared backstage and said there was a telegram for me. It was from my father and it said that he – and my mother – were coming down to see me. Together.

If I were going to go on stage, it was vital that they should see me and, as dutiful parents, decide whether I had made a wise choice. After all, they had seen Olivier, Gielgud and the great French actor Jean Louis Barrault. None of whom would have been seen dead in weekly rep in Minehead.

It seemed that my mother had finally sold the flat on Mount Carmel!

One of the last times I saw my parents together was after they had both sat in the stalls watching me make my stage debut as the youngest detective sergeant in history in a play called *Get Away with Murder*. They said that I hadn't been bad but that it was a bit strange to see a policeman as young as I was.

I later played the wise-cracking son in *Critics' Choice*. The boy's father pays him for writing snappy one-liners such as 'Everything about the play was wooden – apart from one thing and that unfortunately was the scenery.'

Over the next eighteen months, I tried hard to make it as an actor. I auditioned for many parts. I tried to get into the Royal Academy of Dramatic Art in the footsteps of Albert Finney *at el*. My mother told me that I had no hope if I did not go to the audition smartly dressed, and she insisted I turn up in a suit. I felt stiff and it was definitely not the right outfit in which to do one of the speeches from *Romeo and Juliet*.

After the speech, the panel conferred. We had all worked out that only if you were called back to do a second piece in the afternoon did you have a chance.

'We'll be writing to you,' they said. 'Next.'

I knew what that meant. I'd failed. I hadn't even made it to the second round. I walked out of the building and held back the tears. But as soon as I was round the corner, I started to sob. I'd worked as a professional actor on the stage. How could they reject me? But I knew then that my great adventure was over. I was seventeen years old and I knew I'd have to eat humble pie and go to Oxford or Cambridge.

'Of course, it will cost me money,' my father said. Now I was really going to owe him.

Slowly, the tragicomic truth about my mother's relationship with Mr Soussi came out. For three years Soussi had asked her to marry him, but she did not want to give my father the satisfaction of divorcing her. If she were to marry Soussi, she would have to divorce my father, leaving him to marry Evi and, no doubt, continue to Casanova all over the place.

In later years, she always said that I had hated Soussi. So how could she marry him? She couldn't upset me.

But when Evi had had her first child by my father, my mother finally she decided she would marry Soussi. I only have her word for what happened. My mother rang Soussi to tell him the good news. He was delighted. He started making plans for the wedding. But at some point during the next twenty-four hours he had a heart attack and fell down dead.

'It was so sad,' my mother said, 'and tragic.'

Slowly I understood that this was not just a human tragedy but a financial one. Unless she agreed to marry him, Soussi would leave all his considerable estate to his son. As soon as they were man and wife, he would, he promised, change his will in my mother's favour. It was very inconsiderate of him to die before he had had the chance to visit his lawyers.

My mother had the good sense at least to realise that Soussi's son hated her just as much as I hated Soussi. Dennis was not going to give her a penny because that might have been what his father wanted.

Soussi was the third man who had let her down, she complained.

And now I discovered the truth about her first husband. Mr Kertesz was a dashing young man. One day my mother returned from the law office where she was studying much earlier than usual. Her husband had told her he had to work outside the city, so she did not expect to find anyone there. But there were noises. She was scared. It must be burglars. She turned away and made for the front door. It was then that she saw his overcoat lying on the floor. And his shirt. And his trousers. And his shoes.

After years of hearing her own mother complain about her father's infidelities, she began to suspect the worst. She tiptoed to the door of their bedroom and flung the door open.

In their own bed, she told me, 'and with a man'. She wasn't embarrassed by the fact that they were both men but she was outraged that it had happened in her own bed! My father at least had the minor decency to canoodle in offices, hotels or on the premises of ladies of easy virtue.

Kertesz's lover was in fact a soldier. No wonder my mother did not trust men.

'Of course, these days … men are with men all the time.'

She was so ashamed. Her father was so ashamed. Kertesz was so ashamed. Her mother, of course, could never be allowed to find out.

'That was why when your father came along …'

… she had married him. She had been unlucky with her men.

It took me years to realise that she had her reasons, her story, her *life*, and therefore that I should have some sympathy for her. She had given up on my father finally. As she saw it, Mr Soussi was her last chance. After he died, she never wanted to talk about what had happened. I tried more than a few times to ask how she could have left me – not always in anger, but to help me to understand. But she would always avoid the subject. And she never apologised. Sometimes, when she was worried the subject might come up, my mother would go on the attack. How could I, the unjust son, accuse her of being a bad mother? She was the real victim. I couldn't understand. And then she would go all literary on me.

She'd make references to Albert Cohen's tender *Le Livre de Ma Mère – The Book of My Mother*. In Britain, Albert Cohen is not well known; in France, he's seen as a very great writer. My mother inflated him into Shakespeare and Goethe rolled into one, the greatest of writers. The reason was simple. Albert Cohen knew how to be a good son. His book is a hymn of praise to his mother, how she loved him, how she cooked for him, how nothing was too good for him. He felt guilty when he became an important diplomat and helped bring peace to the world because it meant he had less time to devote to Mama. He dedicated all his books to his mother.

Compared to Albert Cohen, I was a lousy son.

My mother was bitter about having to divorce my father, and it was hard for her to bear. She belonged to a generation of women who were made to feel that marriage and their family was all. Slowly, over the years, I grasped that.

Despite all this, I could never love my mother as I had when I was a boy. But if I could never forgive her, I did feel strangely responsible for her. I wanted to be sure that if she had to get a divorce, she would be all right financially. As a psychologist, I now know how easy it is for children to feel that they are to blame when their parents' marriage goes wrong. I had always wanted to make it better. Now that the long saga of my parents' marriage had come to an end, I worried about my mother even if, sometimes, quite often in fact, she made me completely furious.

I would like to record another ironic secret. Melitta's husband, who picked me up at the airport, turned out to have a juicy secret. When they had their first boy, Melitta had wanted to call him Hermann.

Rudi told her that was not possible – and it was not easy to explain. He already had a son called Herman. His daughter, my second cousin Terry, found out before her father died that Rudi had fled from Vienna when the Nazis took Austria over in 1938. Rudi was penniless and decided his best chance of escape was to go into Germany. He managed to get a job in a store which was owned by a woman a few years older than him; they became lovers. The woman became pregnant. She guessed Rudi was Jewish because he was circumcised and helped him flee. Somehow he got to Dunkirk and was evacuated to Britain.

As he was dying, Rudi told his children the truth. They have now tracked down their half brother who is a minor celebrity in Germany. The irony is that the man claims to be the son of a high-ranking Nazi officer.

Chapter 10

Being a Father

B ut I need to backtrack to that awful moment when I realised I would not get into the Royal Academy of Dramatic Art, which I nicknamed the Royal Calamity of Dreadful Art.

If I wanted to go to Oxford, there would, as I say, be humble pie to eat. And I had to eat it in bucketfuls, to consume positively mounds of the tart of humilitude. My father was pleased that I had failed to become an actor and that he had been shown to be the perfect parent. He had been tolerant, helpful, indulgent, not some monster who forced his son to do things the son did not want to do. Good parents supported their children – and hadn't he done just that? My mother tried to get in on that act but she was less convincing. The High Master of St Paul's, Howarth, agreed to give me a reference after one of his staff – whom my father had given money to – put great pressure on him. Howarth, however, was to get a little revenge. He would only give me a reference to Keble College, Oxford, which was then largely known for theology, port and turning out future leaders of the Church of England.

Failing to get into RADA and going to Oxford changed my life for ever. On the third day that I was there, I stopped to look at the map outside Blackwell's bookshop and St John's College. I was lost, and I wasn't the only one. Two American girls were also studying the map. We started chatting. They were from Trinity College, Washington, and they were spending a year in Oxford. One was rather plump and I hardly looked at her. But the other one, Aileen, was very pretty. She became the mother of my children.

Aileen La Tourette had also had a traumatic childhood. Her mother was a fiery French-Irish woman who could be violent. Her father was a distinguished stockbroker and a clever and nice man, but he had a severe alcohol problem. She's written about both her parents in her novels.

After many ups and downs, Aileen and I got married. I was twenty-three and she was six months older.

The curious thing is that she did not see my mother and myself as so estranged – and she certainly didn't believe I was cut off from her.

'You were tight and exclusive,' she told me. 'When we got married, you went shopping with her. On my wedding day we had to worry about picking her up from the hair-dresser. You and she decided that the dinner set we got as a wedding present from my aunt was the wrong one and you changed it without my being there. You were a little conspiracy.'

I can't for a minute dismiss what Aileen has to say, but it was not how I felt at the time or, at least, how I recollect feeling when I look back now.

My parents had had no very clear idea of how a marriage might work. Aileen's parents were still together but far from happy. We in turn needed time to work out how to be married, to have fun together and to find our way to being a couple. We never had that time because Aileen became pregnant. She was very keen to have a baby.

The textbooks claim that unhappy children make bad parents. It is not just that they do not experience love, but that no one passes on to them the skills required to be a good parent. Human beings don't learn skills automatically, whether driving a car or writing Persian poetry or growing prize flowers. We learn how to do these things, even if we have a gift for them, because we receive teaching and training. Being a parent is one of the most complex of all tasks, and yet you are supposed to know how to do it simply because it was once done to you.

Given my experiences – and that I now knew some psychology – I was terrified by the prospect of becoming a father.

After we married, Aileen and I moved to a flat over one of my father's shops in Norbury, south London. After the Berg drama, my father had a brief period when he thrived as a company 'doctor' helping to rescue companies that were on the verge of insolvency. During this short golden spell, he had somehow acquired eleven shops which rented televisions – a business that doesn't exist any more. By 1970 it wasn't going too well and he had had to give up the grand office in Jermyn Street. He and Evi were now living in Brighton where they briefly ran a hostel for Jewish students.

I didn't like living on his turf in Norbury. Aileen and I managed to save some money and we borrowed some more from our parents, and we managed to buy a small flat in Greenwich. By the time we moved in, Aileen was three months pregnant.

Aileen loved being pregnant. She was going to have the

child she had wanted for so long. The boring bits, the getting fat, feeling lethargic, being too involved with it to do anything else, were minor irritations. She was joyful.

For me it was a shock. Sensible young men sowed their wild oats and tried to stay free for as long as possible.

In December 1970, we spent a strange three weeks in Vevey on the shore of Lake Geneva. After leaving Oxford, I had rather miraculously become a screenplay writer and I had been hired by James Mason to write a screenplay of *Jane Eyre*. He put us up in the most expensive hotel in town. The hotel had an enormous Christmas tree that was decorated with real candles. They blazed away, the biggest fire risk ever. Bell boys stood around with hoses, which, given how expensive the rooms were, the hotel could well afford.

We had a magnificent room overlooking the bay. We lolled on the great double bed and I tried to listen to the beating of our unborn child's heart. As Aileen's belly grew and grew, the presence of that baby-to-be became more and more real. It was a time of extraordinary happiness.

Just before the New Year, we took the train back to London. Aileen finally began to be bored by pregnancy and couldn't wait for the birth. We went to natural childbirth classes. In those days, a man was a paragon if he attended even one antenatal class, and I can't claim that I went out of my to go to more. We were told what part we might play in the great event. I felt awe as I listened to the baby's heartbeat amid the gurgle of all the other noises inside her. Inside Aileen there was another human being. Each of us men in the class was given two or three minutes to listen to that throb of life.

We became more and more excited though everyone we knew who had had a baby warned that the little beasts never arrived on time. We painted a blue elephant on one wall because, to be fulfilled, a baby would need to look at an elephant.

One evening Aileen had some dramatic contractions. Then they petered out. The next evening when I came home, she said she had been having contractions all afternoon. I panicked with delight. She told me to calm down. Knowingly, I told her that this was the night. We ate and we tried to read, but it was hard to think about anything else.

Then, suddenly, as Aileen was sitting on the bed, there was a gush and a plop. Her waters had broken. As she sat in the puddle I told her, sagely again, that I knew the baby was coming. I rang for the ambulance and wondered what on earth I would do if Aileen suddenly started to give birth in our flat. Images of myself as a heroic male midwife coursed through my mind. Luckily, the ambulance was there within five minutes to take us to Greenwich District Hospital.

The hospital gave Aileen a hard time. They would not believe her when she said she was very close to giving birth. They insisted on giving her an injection of pethidine to 'relax you, dear' even though Aileen said that she didn't want it. I felt too intimidated by the omniscient nurses and by my own confusion at becoming a father to help her stand her ground. Then they left us alone in a small room.

After an hour we rang the bell because Aileen was sure she was about to pop. She felt the instinct to push. The midwife asked me if I really wanted to attend the birth, and when I said 'yes', she made it very clear this was a peculiar request. Thirty years ago, men were not supposed to be so involved. But I insisted and so I was made to dress like a surgeon.

In the delivery suite, Aileen was finding it hard to keep

the natural breathing rhythm she had been taught in the childbirth classes. The pethidine had left her disorientated. I sat by her side but I could do little more than hold her hand and encourage her. In and out, in and out, I coaxed her like a feeble cox on automatic pilot.

For a while everything seemed to be going well. Aileen was not in too much pain. The head was engaged in the birth canal and starting to come out. I could sense a mounting fever in myself. The head was not moving. I began to be sure that our child would be born speaking and carrying a message. God – though I happen to be an atheist – would trumpet his message through our child.

Nonsense, perfect nonsense, insane nonsense, I knew. And yet the experience was strong and vivid. I couldn't get it out of my head. I concentrated on holding Aileen's hand and mopping her brow. Soon, very soon, our baby would be born.

Suddenly there was a hush of anxiety to the nurses' voices. Was the baby breathing all right? they asked each other. Was the cord tangled? How long was he or she going to be in the birth canal? The baby seemed stuck. Aileen's muscles were far too relaxed because of the pethidine. Those minutes were the most dreadful I have ever lived through. If the baby was stuck too long in the birth canal, there could be brain damage.

Never mind being an atheist, I prayed to God. My mind wouldn't stop flashing up the worst, most disastrous outcomes. Just as I had been convinced a few minutes earlier that the baby would arrive uttering a profound message for humanity, now I was jelly, praying to the God I did not believe in to make everything all right. Behind the surgical mask, I was sweating, fidgeting and somehow managing not to give voice to any of my fears.

I dared not look at Aileen's vagina because I was sure that if I looked, I'd only see disaster.

Eventually, eventually Aileen managed to conquer the pethidine and push the baby out. He was safe. I could have yelled with relief but I just laughed with delight. The voices in my head calmed down as soon as a perfectly formed baby hit life – and screamed. He was washed down, proclaimed male and given to Aileen to hold. We called him Nicholas.

Aileen burst into tears and just kept repeating that he was beautiful. She was right about that. The nurses told us he weighed seven pounds and four ounces. Aileen hugged him, rocked him and cried over him. The nurse announced his length in inches. I was allowed a very brief moment to hold my son and, brief or not, I can't help thinking that that time was incredibly important.

Half an hour after Nicholas was born, the routine of the hospital imposed itself. He was taken off to the nursery and I was told I had to leave. After a final hug, I left Aileen. I walked through the quiet corridors of the hospital. It was 4.30 in the morning. The moment I got out I couldn't contain my delight. I ran all the way up the hill to the block of flats where we lived and rang her parents. They were suitably delighted. As were my own.

My father, of course, had not been present when I was born. My mother told Aileen that she had found the business of giving birth unbearably messy.

In the months that followed, Aileen bore the burden of the parenting – and she was often dead tired. He was more her son than my son.

The partial nature of my relationship with Nicholas became clear one evening when he was about six months old. He was sitting up by then and I was sitting facing him. I had decided to devote a few minutes to being a good daddy and was about to roll a pink plastic ball towards his toes to help develop his coordination.

Suddenly this little baby started to laugh at me.

And laugh and laugh and laugh.

I laughed back.

We sat there, fixed to the spot by these gurgles of laughter, for minute after minute. The laughter kept on bursting, flowing, popping. No joke or cartoon provoked it. Here there was nothing except love and recognition. Sitting in his nappy, ignoring the pink ball I had conscientiously rolled at his toes, my son laughed and laughed at me. And I laughed and laughed at him. Aileen came into the room, saw what was happening and just watched. I didn't notice for ages that she was there.

It was wonderful. There isn't a particular moment, of course, when a child really becomes your child, but there are moments that change you and that you remember having changed you. As we sat there together and laughed, he really became my most precious son.

I was lucky. I have no idea what triggered that laughter. Once I was in it, I was totally there. A 'peak experience' some psychologists would call it. It didn't mean that I became the perfect daddy, Aileen still did more of the child care, but I knew that I was totally committed to my son.

Did my father ever experience such a moment with me? I doubt it – I doubt it very much. Men of his generation were not usually that involved with their children when they were small.

In the three years after Nicholas was born, my marriage had its problems, but then we decided we would have another child. I left my job at Thames Television when Aileen was about four months pregnant because we had decided to go to Greece for at least three months, We rented a cottage in a resort called Tolo in the Peloponnese. Villa Daphne had a room for us, a room for Nicholas and a living room. There was a small rocky garden which looked out over a scrubby field on which just one goat seemed to graze. Fishermen as well as tourists used the beach.

It was off the beaten track and we lived the away-from-it-all idyll. Every morning one of us would write while the other one took Nicholas to the beach. After lunch and a siesta, Nicholas went to the beach with his other parent. I went to Athens one day a week as I had managed to get some commissions to write articles for various magazines.

In the evening we would often listen to Aileen's tummy and the gurgles and kicking of the baby to come.

At the end of November 1974, we turned up at Athens airport. We were a little worried that they might not let Aileen on the plane as she was so pregnant, but airlines were quite tolerant in those days. After the stresses of the first birth in hospital, Aileen had opted to have her second child at home. Her midwife, Miss Church, was a local character in Greenwich. She was midwife to women who were the grand-daughters of women she had delivered previously.

Reuben's birth was less traumatic than Nicholas's. The moment he was born Aileen and I each put a drop of champagne on our fingers and put them to his lips.

Champagne Charlie, we called him.

There wasn't quite such a dramatic moment of bonding but then I held him, cuddled him and changed his nappies far more. I really liked being a father. I'm not pretending for a moment that I have been any kind of perfect parent. My children would smack me were I to make such a fatuous claim, but I don't think they'd argue with two things. I enjoy being a father and I take it seriously.

My father's bursts of anger have left their mark on me. I

can go into what my sons call my raging bull act, but it's pretty rare, is never physical and is usually triggered by something not that personal. Poor service is sometimes a red rag. I once bellowed in a Greek restaurant, 'If you're going to serve us why don't you say so?'

In fact, I sometimes think that one legacy of my father's anger has been to make me too afraid of shouting and confrontation. I am apt to appease.

When I studied psychology at Oxford, there was very little research on fatherhood. As a result of the Second World War there had been some work which showed that children whose fathers were away during the war scored less well on IQ tests and tended to be less well adjusted socially. They were more likely to end up in jail. It does not seem to have changed much. Recently, black clergymen in Boston have claimed that 95 per cent of the delinquents there are fatherless and that being fatherless is at the root of their problems.

Some writers argue that men are incapable of being good fathers. Rosalind Miles, in her provocative *The Children We Deserve*, claims that most men cannot fulfil the basic requirements of parenting. Jealous and sex-obsessed little boys that we are, we cannot give what Miles believes is the most important gift of all, unconditional love.

And even if the old man happens to be there, he is not a simple character. The old man sets up obstacles because, unconsciously, he is so jealous of the child, for once the child is born, the old man will never be No. 1 again, the only object of the mother's adoration. I must say I am not entirely sure what 'unconditional love' means, and I worry that it sounds a very grand phrase. But I think I know – having been a parent and a step-parent – what loving children involves.

Loving them through thick and thin.
Loving them when they are being a pain.
Talking to them.
Never not returning their phone calls.
Buying them things they need.
Buying them things they don't need.
Helping with the homework.
Telling them they look great when they do.
Telling them they look great when they don't.
Not lying to them.
Not bad-mouthing their other parent.
Making sure they know where you are.
Endless practical and emotional support.

James Watson, the son of the great psychologist John B. Watson, told me that the best and closest times he had with his father were when they did carpentry together. I'm not suggesting that doing carpentry is enough to show love, but Watson's son understood that it was a very masculine way of bonding.

Perhaps the most useful psychoanalytic ideas on parenting come from the late D. W. Winnicott. He argued that babies and children do fine as long as they have good enough mothering. Mama did not have to sing nursery rhymes every night to her little one and always feed the infant with extract of sweet honey. Winnicott did not write much about fathering, though he stressed the need for the father to give both the mother and the child emotional support. I have adapted his ideas to develop the concept of good enough mothering and fathering. The basics are very simple.

Be there.

Don't act violently towards your children. The odd smack is fine as long as you are in control of yourself, and they can see that you are in control of yourself.

Don't deny them emotional warmth.

Don't be too inconsistent. But remember that no human being is totally consistent, and don't try for the impossible.

Don't ever be indifferent.

And try not to forget the imbalance of power between you, the parent, and your children.

As for the old wisdom – 'Honour thy father and thy mother that thy days may be long' – well, that is a good thing, undoubtedly, but how curious, and what a shame, that the Bible does not also tell us to honour our children and to protect them because they are so vulnerable.

In any case, the Bible is hardly a guide to good parenting, offering many examples of atrocious parenting. The most obvious is that of Abraham, who is ready to sacrifice Isaac because God tells him to.

My own parents certainly did not tick the good-enough-parent boxes. The hurt they caused me is still with me at times. And when I think about it now, I sometimes feel utterly baffled. Though I've tried to see it their way, and to feel sympathy for their disappointments, in the end they were the parents and I was the child.

Now that I have children I don't see how they could have left me alone.

And they could never make up for that afterwards.

Chapter 11

The Last Secret

The more you live, the less you understand.

By the early 1970s, my father and Evi had three children. He told me it was essential to have a divorce. My mother delayed in every way she could. Partly she did not want to lose him finally, and divorce would be final; partly she believed he was trying to cheat her financially. Her solicitors encouraged her in this belief. Every time my father protested he had lost money, they claimed he had salted thousands or tens of thousands away in Swiss bank accounts.

I realised that my father was not lying, or not too much, and that my mother was very vulnerable. It took seven years for them to agree a divorce, and, during that time, I was often forced to negotiate between them.

'Naturally you must defend your mother,' my father said.

'If only I had resisted your father as a suitor,' my mother said.

I pointed out that she had found Kertesz in bed with a man.

'I found your father in bed with women. And don't forget that Indian secretary,' she added.

At one point, when my mother had gone back on her promise to sign a certain document, I became so exasperated that I threatened to jump off the balcony at the back of Vincent Court. The balcony was only eight feet off the ground. At most I'd twist an ankle.

But I yelled, like my father used to do. And I pleaded.

My threat did the trick. My mother signed.

But the civil divorce was not the end of it. My father also wanted a religious divorce. Otherwise his three other children would be bastards under Jewish law. To pressure me into pressuring her to agree, my father now revealed the last secret. He and Dolly would have been perfectly happy if she had not denied him one essential thing. My mother had been so warped, such a bad wife, that she had had a series of abortions. He had wanted me to have brothers and sisters. But her family influenced her not to have more children. I owed it to him to make sure that Daniel, Raphael and Naomi were not *mamzers*, the Hebrew word for 'bastards', because my mother had denied him the family he wanted.

I never dared confront her with the story of the abortions which must have been both illegal and dangerous in the 1940s and '50s. His pressure worked, and I nagged her to give him the Jewish divorce he wanted.

My mother dressed up for the occasion. To get a religious divorce, you have to petition the court of the rabbis, the Beth Din, which was then housed off the Euston Road. From the outside the building looked like an ordinary office block. The court inside was almost medieval, however. The rabbis wore gowns and the lighting was low. They had to make enquiries with the Romanian authorities and, of course, documents had gone missing since 1939.

Then they declared that the marriage was dissolved. The ceremony was chilling, the death of more than a marriage. It was almost like the death of a soul.

My mother sat in front of them like stone. She answered their questions in a lifeless monotone. I never saw her in such misery, and I remembered how she had looked that first time I saw her off to Israel. Compared to the way she looked now, so deathly, she had been pirouetting then.

My father sent her a note saying he was grateful to her because justice could now be done to his other children.

My mother was now in her late fifties. She could still be attractive, she was still charming, but she saw herself only as a woman who had failed. Three men had let her down. She became depressed and ever more demanding. She took more laxatives, more tranquillisers, saw more doctors. At one time she had three consultants dealing with her eyes, and when they found out that she was playing one off against the other, they lectured her about abusing the National Health Service. 'I am a helpless foreigner' – she delivered the line beautifully to excuse herself when in fact she'd been here for twenty-five years.

She continued to make bad choices. The most dramatic one was when Aileen and I suggested she come to live with us. We had seen a lovely house in Gloucester Circus, a very elegant and expensive part of Greenwich. It had a granny flat. If my mother sold Vincent Court and we sold our house – we had moved from the flat where Reuben was born – we could afford the mansion.

We visited it. My mother liked the house and the granny flat, which gave out on the garden.

'You will be laughing and I will be alone down here,' she worried.

'No, we'll be next door,' Aileen said.

I pointed out that in fact we would be much closer.

I tried to shake her out of that fear, and so did Aileen. But nothing worked. My mother clung to Vincent Court as hard as she had clung to that flat on Mount Carmel. I suspect that she didn't trust me. Perhaps I'd do something crazy like mortgage the house to make a film and then she'd be left homeless.

While we continued to lived in Greenwich, Aileen and I would sometimes walk past that house and just wondered how living there might have changed all our lives.

I think that one of the effects of this is that I've been unable to have proper relationships with Jewish women. As I get older, I find this more and more puzzling. Some of the Jewish women I went out with were never very serious but I sabotaged the relationships very quickly in all cases but one.

At one time I was very much in love with Hanya. She was a fiery, curly-haired Polish girl I'd met in Amsterdam when I was making a film about hijacking. A friend of hers took me to the Festival of Fools, and there I saw Hanya dancing like a magnificent wild woman on a table. I was leaving the next day but I rang her from the airport.

'Ring me next time you're coming,' she said.

I did, and we had an intense affair, but, in the end, I think I was too intense for her at the time. I still have the letter she wrote to me to say that she did not want to continue our affair though she wanted to remain friends. We did, but I got, I am sorry to say, a perfect passive-aggressive revenge. I slept with one of her friends.

As my mother grew older, our relationship did not improve very much.

My relationship with my mother was damaged, and it damaged me and it damaged her.

I didn't have the heart to be really warm to her. I saw her once every week at least, but it was never enough for her. She kept on ringing and saying things like, 'I just wanted to hear your voice.' My children gave her great pleasure and she was a good grandmother to them. In 1980, she turned seventy-six. The misery of the divorce was a little in the past now but she started saying there was no point to her life. She was a useless old woman. Her eyesight was getting worse. Aileen and I took her to the theatre sometimes, but it did little good.

She said that if I were a good son, I'd help her kill herself. I had many friends who were doctors. Surely they could give me some pills. Painless, the end. She could be at peace with her beloved mother and father.

I refused and kept on refusing.

She told me she had written to a group in Switzerland that gave you instructions on how to kill yourself.

I tried to jolly her out of it.

She still had her moments, despite her depression. Aileen took her shopping for shoes when she was eighty. My mother refused to buy sensible shoes, even in old age. She had to have heels because she didn't want to look frumpy. Aileen caught the whole expedition – and a nicer side of my mother – in a touching story she wrote, called 'Echo Shoes', from which I'd like to quote with her permission. My mother, called Ruth in the story, wanted to go to Ferragamo's to buy some stylish shoes.

'Remember Ruth,' she warns her sternly. 'Afterwards we're going to John Lewis to get the Ecco shoes the doctor says you need.'

'O, they are so ugly.' Ruth can find nothing. She wants to cry. She can't remember eating today. Some bread maybe with her coffee. It's so much trouble to cook and the meals the home help makes will poison her if she eats them. Horrible English food her stomach can't digest. Her stomach digests French, Romanian, Hungarian, German, Spanish, Italian, all the languages she speaks. Really she should have been an interpreter. Only English she can speak but not digest.

'There's the taxi. Let's get this show on the road,' Jackie says impatiently. What has the old bat lost now? Why does she have to fumble and claw at things and make such a big production out of everything? It's exactly like getting a baby ready to go out. A nightmare. At least babies pretty much pass out once they hit the fresh air. This one goes on complaining.

Eventually, in Aileen's story, Ruth is forced to buy shoes with no heels as opposed to the glamorous ones she really wants by Ferragamo or Chanel, like those that she still keeps in her wardrobe. Aileen caught beautifully the disappointed debutante at the ball that my mother remained, in part, well into her eighties.

My relationship with my father changed as his and Evi's children grew up. It had never been as intense as that with my mother. I'd needed his approval when I was younger, but as I started to make TV programmes and publish books, I needed his approval less and less. As I mentioned, he refused to speak to me for a year when my first book was published. Aileen's mother made the peace between us but it remained an uneasy one.

When my father started to become frail the balance of power between him and Evi also changed. She had been the weak one throughout their marriage. Now he'd spend hours sitting in an armchair doing nothing. My last memory of him – a week before he died – is of Evi holding his penis while he peed. It was touching. And I should make clear that time has healed my anger towards her, and I know that Benjamin was neither an ideal nor an easy husband. He was too disappointed for that.

When my father was buried, Evi and Dolly met for the first time since the 1960s. They were polite to each other. I wept for my father, wept for his death and wept for the fact that the young man who was so promising, clever and energetic died in a country he never understood. From Mount Carmel to Streatham Cemetery – a strange journey.

I thought that my father's death would hit my mother hard. It did so less than I had expected it to. She hated losing her sight and she could no longer read or do her gymnastic exercises. She became more depressed, completely wrapped up in her own misery. I told myself that I really should forgive her. I tried to talk to her about what had happened but still she avoided the subject. The closest she came to apologising was to insist that I had to understand that Benjamin had made her go to Israel. I let it drop.

The last time I saw my mother was on 22 March 1997. I took her for a walk round Regent's Park. She complained that she was a prisoner in Vincent Court. She was a useless person living out a useless existence. I should be a good son and get her the pills so she could kill herself.

I told her not to be so silly. She had me, she had her grandchildren, she still had amusing stories to tell. I became exasperated. I had a meeting to go to so I put her in a taxi to take her home. I was relieved to get away.

She didn't ring me the next day. So the day after, I rang in the morning. There was no answer. That was not unprecedented – she still liked to go to Selfridges for hours at a time. When I rang again that evening there was still no answer. I knew she took lots of sleeping pills, and so I was able to tell myself that she was snoring away under the influence. It was only the next morning when she still didn't answer the phone that I raced round to Vincent Court.

The door was on the chain. I had to call the police to break in through the back door. She was lying on the carpet in her bedroom. She had taken pills and cognac. She never recovered consciousness.

My mother had always asked me to promise I would have her buried in Israel. I kept that promise. Five days later, at the cemetery in Haifa, I was astonished that nearly a hundred people turned up. These were not just family but friends – mainly my mother's friends who were, as she had been, old now. Most of them loved living in Israel and were sad that she had gone back to London in 1970. They were jolly men and women. One of the men who came to pay his last respects was Mr Kertesz, who forty-nine years earlier had been caught in bed with a soldier.

I had one last duty to perform. At the cemetery the officials showed me her body. I had to confirm that it was indeed my mother in the white burial shroud. When I stated that it was indeed the body of Dolly Cohen, they placed her in the ground.

At my mother's funeral, I learned, thanks to my cousin Lydia, what should have been completely obvious. Mr Soussi had been not 'just a friend' but my mother's lover. My mother had often mocked Soussi. He was, of course, in love with her, but men had been in love with her since she was sixteen. Nothing had happened. The very idea was ridiculous.

At the funeral, I pretended that I had known all along, but I hadn't – funny, really, since I like to think that I am worldly wise. I was angry at myself and angry at my mother. She'd had the last laugh from the grave, and I felt like a complete idiot.

My father, I discovered later, had known about her affair with Soussi from very early on but had said nothing. He had agreed with her that I should not be told the truth.

When I returned to London, I went to her solicitor to hear her will. I told myself that she was capable of pulling another surprise like she had when I was a teenager. She always told me that she would leave me everything, but I wouldn't have been astonished to find she had left her money to someone else.

I was wrong. Her will ran for only a single sentence. 'I leave all my real and other property to my beloved son, David.' She had made the will out twenty years before she died – and never altered it.

This is not just a book about my childhood and psychological theory. It is also, necessarily, a book about my mother – if she had not left me, I wouldn't have had so much to say about my childhood or psychological theory. My mother always wanted her *Livre de Ma Mère*, but we rarely give people precisely the gifts they desire. This, then, isn't quite the book my mother would have wanted, but it is very much about her. And here is the final ambivalence. Part of me wishes she could read it so that she would know how I really felt; part of me is glad that she can't because it would hurt her.

I hope that both of my parents are resting in peace.

Postscript

Because I became a psychologist, I could hardly have told this story without involving the grand old bearded guru who first told us that half the middle-class children in Vienna had been abused by their parents – and then changed his mind.

Freud argued in 1905 that his patients kept on telling him of abuse they had suffered. A few years later, he said these were not real memories of real events, but desires. On the couch, his patients 'recalled' things they wished had happened, dreams of the Oedipus complex fulfilled.

Freud also believed that his mother's love gave him the confidence to be, as he wrote, a 'conquistador'. If she hadn't adored him, he would never have had the chutzpah to conquer the mysteries of the psyche. But her love also made Freud jealous, and without that jealousy he probably wouldn't have had the insight to 'invent' the Oedipus complex.

If your mother doesn't love you, it will affect you from womb to tomb, according to psychologists. You're

very likely to become deprived, depraved and delinquent. How many axe murderers say they basked in
their mother's love?

In 1946, one of Freud's followers, the psychoanalyst
John Bowlby, wrote a paper which argued that a group
of forty-four juvenile thieves had all suffered 'maternal
deprivation'. Starved of mother love, these youths were
doomed to become criminals and spend their lives in
jail. (I interviewed him and the image that has stayed
with me is of him and his bowler hat – the perfect
English gentleman shrink.) Bowlby's ideas became
orthodoxy. For example, Sure Start, the UK government's programme for children, aims to make sure that
all children get exactly that – an emotionally sure start
to their lives.

Feminists often complain that psychoanalysis
blamed mothers for any problems in how children
develop. They have a point. Other schools of psychology
are less likely to pillory mothers. While psychoanalysis
concentrates on understanding thoughts and feelings,
behaviourists like John B. Watson and Burrhus Skinner
argued that psychology should focus on what people
actually do, their observable behaviour.

The founder of behaviourism, John B. Watson (who
also founded modern advertising as we know it) wrote
a bestseller on child care in which he stressed the
importance of fathers. Watson was the Dr Spock of his
day. He claimed he could do better than the Jesuits.
They boasted that if they were given a child till the age
of seven, that child would be 'theirs', a faithful follower,
for the rest of its life. Watson, a devout atheist, boasted
back that that was unscientific peanuts. With the help

of scientific psychology, he could turn a kid into a salesman, a bus driver, an acrobat, a deadbeat or a strong and confident personality.

I have always had a soft spot for John B. Watson. He was born in Greenville, North Carolina, in 1878. His own delinquent father, Pickens, ran away from home to canoodle with a Native American woman when John B. was ten. The boy was devastated at first but he recovered quite quickly. He started to shine at school but even after he went to study under the great minds at the University of Chicago, he remained rather insecure. For the rest of his life, for instance, Watson found it hard to sleep in the dark and always had to have a night light on.

In later life Pickens would sometimes turn up at the offices of the advertising agency, J. Walter Thompson, where his son had become Vice President. The old man would try to touch his rich and now famous son for a few bucks for booze. Watson usually forked out, but he despaired of Pickens. And the great psychologist admitted that he was surprised by how hard he found it to be angry with the father who had left him.

Is it an accident that Watson, who had been abandoned by his father, should become so interested in child psychology and what makes a good parent?

Is it an accident that I'm fond of Watson and interested in the psychology of parenting?

Hardly, but it took me a long time to admit that – and Watson never did. Curiously, psychologists don't like to admit that their own childhood experiences may have attracted them to the subject or to particular aspects of it. My teachers at Oxford in the late 1960s would have discouraged any such outrageous idea because psychology was meant to be objective and scientific; it was certainly not supposed to tell you how to be an agony aunt or how to live your life better. Watson paid dearly for his boastfulness. His oldest son became a Freudian psychiatrist and killed himself.

Some doctors and philosophers were curious about how children develop and how that can be 'improved' long before there was a science of psychology. At the end of the eighteenth century, a child was found in southern France who seemed to have been living with wolves. The Wild Boy of Aveyron was reckoned to be seven years old, but he couldn't speak, couldn't walk properly and had no idea how to use a plate or a cup. Jean Marc Itard, the doctor who tried to treat him, wanted to know if a child who had been so damaged could be taught to speak and to behave normally. Itard tried very hard but, essentially, he failed. By the age of seven the wild boy was too damaged to be helped. Other studies of so-called 'feral children' have tended to be as pessimistic.

Such extreme deprivation is rare but it still happens. A girl in America was brought up in one room by her parents, kept in nappies and in the dark till she was in her teens. Channel 4 did a study of children in Moscow and St Petersburg who were abandoned by their parents and had to fend for themselves on the streets.

But what is far more common than leaving children to grow up with wolves, keeping them in the dark or even Satanic child abuse is the common domestic variety of child abuse.

Carl Rogers, one of the most famous psychotherapists of the mid-twentieth century, was the founder of humanist psychotherapy. He called patients 'clients', believed in giving them total attention and what he called 'unconditional personal regard', and in listening intently to what they said. Rogers was, like Freud, well aware that children were hit and sexually molested by their parents but he too did not pursue this 'scandal'. Rogers' thinking was based on far more research than Freud's. Freud only ever treated one young patient, Little Hans, who was terrified of horses – the horses reminded him of his father – but the child had not been abused by his father. Or a horse. Rogers on the other hand talked to many abused children when he was in charge of research for a children's charity in Rochester, New York, in the 1930s. Nevertheless, he did not seek much publicity for his 'shocking' findings. In 1938, Rogers stopped studying children and set up as a therapist for adults.

The last thirty years have seen many cases of religious cults that are led by a charismatic – but fundamentally seedy guru – who presides over rampant orgies. I've talked to victims of this kind of abuse and they often have truly bizarre memories. I have heard tales of praying in the nude and dancing in the nude for the greater glory of God. 'And then the older men told them to take off their clothes and kiss them for the Lord wanted them to engage in sex acts.' The established Churches tell you that such things are not mentioned in the Bible, but the cults claim that the establishment is lying. 'If you know how to read the secret texts and have been initiated into the secret knowledge, you'll see Jesus wanted us to do this.' I've

made films on the Order of the Solar Temple and
investigated the Children of God, both cults that
involved such abuse.

When finally the world woke up to the reality of
child abuse, research tended to focus on physical and
sexual abuse. And there is evidence of a vicious circle.
In a film I made for Channel 4 in 1991, I reported that
one-third of all child abusers were themselves abused
as children.

Being hurt hurts for the rest of your life.

The important question is: how can one help children
who have been abused to recover? Many interventions
have been tried – art therapy, cognitive behaviour
therapy, simply talking to a good therapist, anger
management, family therapy and the one which
makes the mind boggle most, insult therapy. Here the
therapist whacks it verbally to the client, telling him or
her that he or she is a pathetic jelly who needs to
pull his or her socks up. It works for some people
apparently. A great deal depends on the intensity of
the abuse. As I said at the start, I was abused but not
physically or sexually. I have no idea how I would
have reacted – what my life would have been like – if
I had suffered that.

One thing I have learned from this book is that it is
worth writing it all down and – perhaps this is a better
way of putting it – writing it all *out* in order to defuse
some of the hurt and anger. I'm hardly the first person
to suggest this, but I know that it has helped me. And,
if you have had the misfortune to have gone through
what I went through, or to have felt as I did, I hope that
it has helped you.